The Mad Science of Golf

On moving past golf industry hype and learning to play better golf

Philip Moore

authorHOUSE®

AuthorHouse™
1663 Liberty Drive, Suite 200
Bloomington, IN 47403
www.authorhouse.com
Phone: 1-800-839-8640

First published by AuthorHouse 11/19/2007

ISBN: 978-1-4259-5631-8 (sc)
ISBN: 978-1-4259-5630-1 (hc)

Printed in the United States of America
Bloomington, Indiana

This book is printed on acid-free paper.

I wish to emphasize that there are no secrets to golf.

- Ernest Jones

Special Thanks to Judi
My hard working editor,
wife & best friend
I Love you

Contents

Forward

Introduction

QUESTIONS you should be asking about YOUR GOLF CLUBS

QUESTIONS you should be asking about YOUR GOLF SWING

QUESTIONS you should be asking about PLAYING BETTER GOLF

Conclusion

Forward

Why I wrote this little book

I'm a clubmaker and I wrote this book as a gift to my customers. To thank them for giving me the opportunity to build their golf clubs and for trusting my guidance.

Acquiring a properly fit set of golf clubs is an important step, but only one step toward becoming a better golfer. I'm hoping, through sharing a few of the discoveries I have made over the past 40 years, I can help my friends better understand the game, get the most out of their new equipment, and move more quickly down the path to better golf.

Phil Moore

Introduction

It's time to see things differently

The average golfer today is scoring no better than the average golfer 30 years ago. Even with all the advances in equipment technology, the average handicap is still the same. This is a fact that golf club manufacturers obviously don't promote. Their usual response is, *"Due to the continual influx of new golfers, the average handicap will always remain high"*.

Well, there have always been new golfers and there always will be new golfers. The undeniable fact is that today's average golfer, playing with far superior equipment, is scoring no better than the average golfer did 30 years ago. *That's because golf is not about technology.* Regardless of how *high-tech* the equipment becomes, golf will always be a simple *low-tech* game. Golf will always be more of an art than a science.

When I refer to the *science* of golf, I'm referring to the study of equipment and swing mechanics. Golfers are drawn to these areas because they believe lower scores are achieved primarily through purchasing better equipment and developing a better swing. Based on everything they've heard or read from the golf industry, this would appear to be the logical assumption. The golf industry, however, is more interested in making money than lowering handicaps. Through hyping the value of *better* equipment and a *better* swing, a great deal of money can be made through selling golf clubs, lessons, books, DVDs, magazines and training aids.

Unfortunately, with regards to either the swing or equipment, there's not even agreement among experts as to what *better* might be. Don't you find it curious that you could take lessons from three different, highly successful PGA teaching professionals and get three different opinions about what you need to do to *improve* your golf swing?

Which one is right? Is it possible they're all right? It is possible, because there are many ways to play golf well. Just take a look at the swings of the top 100 players in the world. They're all different. Hall of Fame golf instructor John Jacobs once said, *"One reason I have always thought that golf can be such a difficult game is simply that there are so many ways to play it correctly."*

How about equipment? Which are the *better* golf clubs? That also depends on whom you ask. Again, take a look into the bags of the top 100 players in the world. It's unlikely you'll find two playing with the exact same 14 clubs. It's not just that these players *swing* differently, they play the game differently. They also have different ideas about what a golf club should feel and look like.

You might be thinking that the top 100 players in the world are all playing with golf clubs that perfectly fit their individual swing. That sounds logical, but if that were true, why are they continually changing golf clubs? Why don't they just keep playing with the clubs that, supposedly, perfectly fit their swing?

While the value science offers to the game is real, it's inherently limited. In fact, when you become overly concerned with either equipment or swing mechanics, improvement becomes almost impossible. The more you study equipment, the more you'll believe that the equipment you're using is not good enough. Furthermore, it's never going to be good enough. You'll always feel it's holding you back. The same applies to swing mechanics. The more you study your golf swing, the more you'll believe that it's the cause of all of your problems.

The truth is you'll never allow yourself to improve because you'll never believe your equipment or swing mechanics warrant it.

Sure, better fitting equipment or a beneficial swing change can help, but only to a point. After that, you'll find yourself joining the rest of the golfers stuck in the world of *mad science,* where the quest for improvement evolves into an endless pursuit of another swing tip or better equipment.

George Bernard Shaw wrote, *"Progress is impossible without change, and those who cannot change their minds cannot change anything."* If you want to improve in golf, you'll need to change how you perceive the *process of improvement.* You'll need to *reprogram* your thinking.

Through a series of simple questions and answers, I'm going to offer you a different perspective on your golf clubs, your golf swing, and how to play better golf.

The first step to improvement is *learning to see things differently.* Let's get started.

PART ONE

QUESTIONS
you should be asking about
YOUR GOLF CLUBS

Some players are never satisfied unless they are buying new clubs…
This is not good for the player, but it is quite good for the clubmaker.

- James Braid
  Five-time British Open Champion
  Between 1901 and 1910

Is the modern golf club a high-tech piece of equipment?

No.

A golf club has only three components: a head, a shaft and a grip. That's it. Each component is mass-produced, usually overseas, with manufacturing tolerances that would never be considered *high-tech*. In fact, I believe the most high-tech aspect of a golf club is the marketing. I find it amazing that year after year marketing departments are able to convince golfers to keep buying expensive new golf clubs.

In addition to not being high tech, modern golf clubs are also not built one at a time by master club makers, as depicted in advertisements. The days of the handcrafted wooden clubheads are long gone. **Today, golf club components are designed for easy assembly and manufacturers build their clubs in a manner similar to an assembly line.** Production is not slowed by mandatory compliance with rigid industry standards because there are no industry standards. To produce a *legal* golf club, the manufacturer need only stay within the guidelines set forth by the governing bodies of golf, the United States Golf Association (U.S.G.A.) and The Royal & Ancient Golf Club of St. Andrews, Scotland (R&A). Detailed specifications and the degree of club-to-club consistency are left completely to the discretion of the individual manufacturer.

In other words, there's no rule that says a 9-iron has to be a certain length and have a certain loft. One manufacturer might decide that a 9-iron should be 36 inches long and have a loft of 44 degrees. And that's fine. Another manufacturer might decide that a 9-iron should be

37 inches long and have a loft of 40 degrees. That's also fine. Unfortunately, the result is two legal clubs, both identified as a 9-iron, which will perform very differently. In the golf club industry, that's perfectly okay.

The same lack of industry standards holds true for shaft flex, shaft torque, lie angle, head weight and grip size. Each manufacturer creates their own standards. Can this lead to confusion? Continuously. One manufacturer's stiff flex 7-iron could have the same specifications as another manufacturer's regular flex 8-iron.

Even the club specifications from the same manufacturer can vary substantially.

For example, if you were to buy ten supposedly identical *high-tech* drivers from a leading manufacturer, removed the heads and measured the specifications, you'd discover that the ten heads weren't identical at all. Although the heads were identically marked and very expensive, you'd find variances in the weight, loft, face angle, face thickness, lie angle and location of the center of gravity. Often the variances won't be significant, but sometimes they will be. *High-tech?*

Now I admit that in recent years leading manufacturers have tightened their controls. Even with overseas manufacturing, assembly line production, and a lack of industry standards, they produce a good product. Not high-tech, but acceptable. *Considering the prices they charge, that's really nice.*

When you play well with a particular golf club, it's because the specifications of that particular golf club happen to fit your swing at that given time. **Regardless of what you might hear from manufacturers, today the magic lies in *golf club fitting* not *high-tech design***

Why are brand name golf clubs so expensive?

Advertising.

The brand name golf club companies that design and market their own equipment are often referred to as OEM's (Original Equipment Manufacturers). While the cost to manufacture golf clubs is relatively inexpensive (because it's done almost entirely overseas), the marketing costs are enormous. An effective global advertising campaign is not cheap. Neither is paying the top players throughout the world millions of dollars to play your equipment.

The marketing costs obviously have to be passed along to the consumer, which is why purchasing brand name golf clubs is expensive. *You're paying for their advertising.* You're led to believe, however, that the added cost is justified because you're also paying for the research, development and precision manufacturing that's necessary to produce such a *high-tech* piece of equipment. *Regardless of what they say – you are paying for their advertising.*

As long as OEM's continue to budget huge amounts of money for marketing, their clubs will continue to be expensive. It's simply a function of business. But that's their problem, it doesn't have to be your problem. If you're not interested in paying a lot of money for advertising, don't buy brand name clubs. It's that simple.

If you'd like quality equipment, but don't want to pay OEM prices, you have two options. The first option is to buy last year's model. Generally, new designs sell at a premium price for a year to 18 months. As soon as the *massively hyped* new design is introduced, the price of the old model drops significantly. That's good news because generally the old model is just as good as (and sometimes even better than) the new model. The downside is that you might have trouble getting the old design built to your exact specifications.

Your second option - *and far better choice* - is to visit your local club-maker. The same overseas foundries that are producing components for OEM's are also producing components for club makers all over the world. The better club makers use only high quality heads, shafts and grips, and do a superior job in fitting. And, because of their limited overhead, they're able to sell their clubs for considerably less than what you'd pay a retailer of brand name products.

Certainly, some club makers are better than others, just as some OEM's are better than others. You'll need to do a little research, but your time will be well spent. A good clubmaker will save you money, do wonders for your game, and will always be there to answer your never ending questions.

If you're having trouble finding a quality clubmaker I'd suggest contacting *The Professional Clubmakers Society* (www.proclubmakers.org 1-800-548-6094). It's a reputable worldwide organization. Their certified club makers have been tested for both their knowledge and skill in all aspects of club building.

Can anything else that really matters be done to a golf club?

No.

For a golf club or golf ball to be deemed *legal* or *conforming*, it must conform to the guidelines set forth by the two ruling bodies of golf (U.S.G.A. and R&A). These two governing bodies are justifiably concerned with protecting the integrity of golf. For example, they don't get too excited about a new golf ball that your 10 year-old daughter can hit 400 yards. *We should all support their efforts.*

The U.S.G.A. handicapping system is based on the player using only *conforming* golf clubs. Serious amateur golfers would never think of using an illegal golf club because they would be unable to establish a legitimate handicap. A professional golfer using an illegal club in tournament play would be disqualified.

As a result, the market for *non-conforming* golf clubs is going to be quite limited. If a manufacturer plans on staying in business, it has to keep its designs within the legal guidelines. This presents a problem. While minor design changes seldom offer a meaningful improvement in performance, major design changes often result in a non-conforming golf club.

So if manufacturers continue to produce only legal golf clubs, what can they really do with their designs that hasn't already been done? That's a really good question, and the answer is... not much. Manufacturers will always be stuck in a give and take mode - *a never-ending juggling act.* Significant design changes will always result in a club that offers improved performance in one area and decreased performance in another.

For example, when manufacturers introduced over-sized titanium fairway metals, they hyped the benefits of the *expanded sweetspot.* The larger heads were indeed more forgiving and they worked great off the tee. Unfortunately, these heads had a *significantly higher center of mass* and when used off the fairway most golfers couldn't get the ball properly elevated. Furthermore, the large clubheads were almost useless from poor fairway lies. The negatives actually out-weighed the positives.

Designers responded with a wave of low profile, sole weighted, low center of gravity designs. The hype over *expanded sweetspot* was replaced with hype about the benefits of a *low center of gravity.* These new fairway metals were much easier to hit off the fairway, but they were not as effective off the tee, or when the ball was sitting up in high rough. Their shallow face left little margin for error and produced a higher percentage of pop-ups. As always, with the positives come the negatives.

So what does this all mean? **It means that if you've been waiting for some future advance in golf club design to dramatically improve the quality of your game, you can forget about it.** It's not going to happen. The ruling bodies of golf have *thankfully* tied the manufacturers' hands.

Just accept the fact that everything that can be done to significantly improve the performance of a golf club has already been done. Instead of looking for a miracle golf club (that you'll never find), look for clubs that better fit your game. Those clubs are available right now and they're all you'll ever need.

How much better are golf clubs really getting every year?

That depends on how you define "better".

Manufactures claim their golf clubs are *better* every year because the designs are superior and the components are more expensive.

Most golfers, however, define a *better* golf club as one which will produce lower scores. With that definition, you'd have to conclude that golf clubs are not getting *better* at all.

If each year the newest *high tech design* in golf clubs was able to save you just *one stroke per round*, you could improve through doing nothing more than buying new golf clubs. Every year your handicap would *automatically* drop by a stroke.

That obviously will not happen. Even though golf clubs are redesigned each year, they will never offer the average golfer a meaningful benefit in performance. This is because, as I mentioned on previous pages, the manufacturers have to stay within the design guidelines established by the governing bodies of golf.

So, if performance driven marketing has hit a wall, how can manufacturers convince golfers to continually purchase expensive new golf clubs? *This is where the marketing department jumps in.* Manufacturers juggle their designs every year in an effort to come up with a new selling point. They have to. What's hot is usually very hot, but only for a short period of time. *As soon as golfers discover that they don't score any better with their new clubs than they did with their old clubs, they start looking elsewhere.*

The good news (for manufacturers) is that golfers love to buy new golf clubs. Soon, someone will get golfers excited about a hot new concept, and the rest of the industry will jump on the bandwagon. R & D departments have become market driven. They know how to spot a potentially hot selling point and they know how to get new designs to the market quickly.

A few of the most successful selling points in the past have been titanium, graphite, oversized, low center of gravity, perimeter weighting, expanded sweet spot, bi-metal technology, spring-face technology and adjustable weighting.

Designer name association has also become a strong selling point. Manufacturers like this angle because it can't be immediately duplicated by the competition. Certain designer's names have been positioned to represent unparalleled quality. Therefore, a clubhead stamped with that designer's name is supposedly worth the considerable added cost. *More hype.*

Whenever you hear of a new hot selling point, try to figure out the downside. There's always a downside. You're not going to hear anything about it, but it's going to be there. For example, when oversized titanium driver heads were first introduced, all you heard about was how much more *forgiving* they were. No mention was made about how the larger clubhead would cause the shaft to twist more during the downswing – *creating problems the golfer never had before.* When oversized iron heads were being hyped as having an *expanded sweetspot,* no mention was made as to how difficult it would be to use these irons from poor fairway lies or out of the rough.

Just remember, improved performance in one area always leads to some degree of decreased performance in another. I've found that when there's no downside the benefit tends to be pure hype. Such was the case with all the madness that centered on the *spring-face effect* of oversized titanium drivers.

During testing, an accidental discovery was made. Balls were rebounding off the face of oversized titanium drivers with more velocity than expected. After researching the matter, it was found that the additional ball speed was due to the elastic nature of the thin titanium faces. At impact, the ball would flatten against the face of the driver and the thin titanium face would deflect inward. Due to its elastic nature, the face would recover (snap back to its original form) faster than the ball would recover. As a result of this *snapping back,* more energy was transferred to the ball and the ball would launch off the face at a slightly higher velocity. Also, because of the face deflecting inward, the ball wouldn't compress or deform as much as it had in the past. Less compression meant that less energy was lost by the ball at impact and that also resulted in higher launch velocity. This phenomenon was soon referred to as the *trampoline effect* or the *spring-like effect* of the titanium clubface.

Marketing departments hyped this new discovery to death. Suddenly oversized titanium drivers were not only more forgiving, they hit the ball farther! Phenomenal (and completely unfounded) claims of added distance were being reported everywhere. While there appeared to be no downside, the actual benefit to the *average golfer* was, unfortunately, imperceptible. To receive any noticeable benefit from the *spring like effect* of a thin titanium face, the golfer must make square and centered contact with clubhead speed well over 100 miles per hour. That's a talent that the average golfer certainly does not have.

Before the matter got any further out of hand, in 1998 the USGA thankfully stepped in and imposed a limit as to how fast a ball could rebound off a clubface. The hype over *spring face technology* soon faded and marketing departments once again had to start looking elsewhere.

Just because golf clubs look different every year doesn't mean they're getting better. *If they didn't look different golfers wouldn't keep buying them.*

I define a *better* golf club as one with which you have the *potential* to make square and centered contact and achieve a playable trajectory a *higher percentage of time.* You'll seldom be lucky enough to find that club on a shelf, but it can be acquired through working with a qualified clubfitter.

Do test results really prove that I'll hit the ball significantly farther and straighter with newer golf clubs?

No.

Some manufacturers like to test golf clubs on mechanical swing machines and then advertise the results as a proven fact - inferring that golfers will experience the same results as the machine.

The fact is that under test conditions, golfers will often experience results exactly opposite of those from a mechanical swing machine.

For example, when a machine is used to test and compare two identical driver heads, one with a 44-inch graphite shaft and one with a similar 48-inch graphite shaft, the driver with the longer shaft will hit the ball, on the average, slightly farther. The results will always be the same.

When the same test is given to golfers, not all of them will hit the driver with the longer shaft farther. Many will be unable to handle the extra 4 inches of length. Their average drive will actually be longer with the shorter shafted driver because they're able to make *square and centered contact* more often. For these golfers the results were exactly opposite of those from the mechanical swing machine.

The machine, unlike a golfer, can be mechanically adjusted so the clubface makes consistent square and centered contact with the ball *regardless of the shaft length.* The better machines can also be adjusted to produce a *specific angle of approach* that will optimize the performance of a particular clubhead. **In other words, through extending the shaft length and altering the angle of approach, a mechanical swing machine can make almost any clubhead appear to be more than it is.**

Unfortunately, technicians can't simply adjust the swing of a real golfer to perfectly compliment the specifications of a golf club. No matter how great the test results were from the swing machine, there's no telling how a golfer will respond to the look, feel and specifications of a particular golf club.

I was once approached by a right-handed weekend golfer who continually sliced his driver. He never practiced and had no interest in taking lessons. He just wanted to know if there was a driver that might help reduce his slice. I noticed his driver had a slightly open face angle (at address the face of the driver was actually aimed to the right of the target), so I had him try a demo driver with a similar shaft and a two-degree closed face angle (at address the face of the driver was aimed well left of the target). Amazingly, he said his slice got worse. From a physics stand point there is absolutely no reason for this to happen. On a mechanical swing machine it would never happen. When I had him hit a few balls on the range I noticed that he opened the face of the demo driver at address. When I asked why he did this, he responded, *"I can't stand looking at the face aiming toward left field. I'm afraid I'm going to hook it!"*

That's the difference between a golfer and a swing machine. A swing machine doesn't think and it has no fears. It also doesn't care how long a golf club is, what a golf club feels like or what a golf club looks like.

Is the modern equipment the primary reason today's professional golfers hit the ball farther and score lower?

No.

The best players in the world are better than ever. The primary reason, according to golf club manufacturers, is that today's players are using far superior equipment. That's *hype*, but we've heard it so often, for so long, that we've all come to believe it.

Whenever a great player hits an exceptionally long drive it's always because of the hot new driver or hot new ball. We listen to television commentators continually debate on what can be done to curb the incredible influence of the golf club technology. We read that the new equipment has made the old courses obsolete.

The hype just goes on and on.

The PGA Tour kicked-off the 2003 season with the Mercedes Championship at the Plantation course in Kapalua Hawaii. That year a strange thing happened. The winds shifted. Downhill holes that were designed to be played into the strong prevailing wind were suddenly being played with the wind at the players back! This, of course, resulted in numerous huge drives, well over 400-yards. The golf club and golf ball manufacturers, of course, ignored the wind factor and hyped the occurrence as further proof of the incredible influence of technology.

The following year, the prevailing wind pattern returned and there were no huge 400-yard drives. Did that mean the newer balls and clubs weren't as good? The manufacturers had no comment.

While all the hype over equipment has resulted in billions of dollars in sales, equipment is not the primary reason professional golfers are hitting the ball farther.

Today's touring professionals hit the ball a lot farther *primarily* because they swing the clubhead a lot faster, the fairways are a lot harder, the golf balls are better, and they use equipment that *better fits* their individual swing.

Now that statement is not going to sell a lot of $500 drivers, so you're not going to hear it advertised on television. You're also not going to read about it in your favorite golf magazine, because your favorite golf magazine relies on the steady flow of advertising dollars from equipment manufactures. *Business is business.*

So how about scoring? Are today's touring professionals scoring lower simply because the fairways are harder, they swing the clubhead faster and their equipment better fits their swing? No. **Today's touring professionals are scoring lower because they have to in order to successfully compete. Today there's a much higher level of competition because golf has become a global game with huge financial incentives.**

Skyrocketing prize money and enormous endorsement contracts have made the best players in the world extremely wealthy. They live in huge estates, travel the world in private jets, mingle with celebrities and enjoy a truly glamorous lifestyle.

In the past, almost all of the top golfers were from the United States. Today, that's no longer the case. There are now tens of thousands of players around the world willing to do whatever it takes to get their piece of the pie. Exceptionally talented players from such countries as Argentina, Korea, Canada, New Zealand, Fiji, Sweden, South Africa,

Australia, Spain, Germany, India, and Paraguay are showing up on the PGA Tour and winning.

Furthermore, these talented young players come to the tour seasoned with years of high level competition coupled with extensive physical and mental conditioning. In the past, this was certainly not the case. In fact, there was a time *not that long ago* when a good portion of the PGA Tour was made up of out-of-shape smokers who spent as much time in the cocktail lounge as they did on the driving range.

I'm not trying to downplay the obvious fact that today's players have benefited by the technological advances in equipment. Advances in technology (especially in precise custom fitting and ball design) have, without question, had an impact on the game. *The degree of impact, however, has been grossly exaggerated in an effort to sell golf clubs.*

While the better equipment has certainly helped, the truth is that it's only been the icing on the cake. The higher level of competition has forced players to learn how to score better. Better equipment does not *force* lower scoring, competition does.

How come touring professionals are scoring lower, but the average golfer isn't?

The average golfer doesn't know how to score lower and doesn't have to.

Even with the advantage of the newest equipment and computer enhanced video golf instruction, the average golfer today is scoring no better than the average golfer 30 years ago. The average handicap is the same.

Why?

First of all, the average golfer *misperceives* the process of improvement. He or she has been taught by the golf industry that lower scores are realized through purchasing *better* equipment and developing a *better* golf swing. That hasn't proven to be true.

Furthermore, the average golfer has no *tangible incentive* to improve. Unlike the professional, if the average golfer doesn't learn to score better, he won't lose his job and he won't lose millions of dollars in endorsement contracts.

If you offered a lifetime 20-handicap golfer five million dollars to drop his handicap to 15, the odds are he'd find a way to do it. Like today's touring professional, he'd be forced to look past his equipment and his golf swing and focus entirely on learning *how to score lower.*

Unfortunately, no one is going to offer you five million dollars to drop your handicap by five strokes. And if you don't improve, nothing in your life if going to change for the worse. So you'll just keep working on your swing, keep buying new equipment, and never score any better.

Are the newest golf clubs always more forgiving and easier to play with?

No.

There's no doubt that some head designs make the game *easier to play* for the average golfer. For example, high-lofted drivers, low-profile fairway metals, hybrid clubs, low center of gravity iron heads, and perimeter weighted putters make the game easier for the average golfer to play.

There is, however, nothing *high-tech* or even *modern* about those designs. They've been around for decades. Yet they're commonly given a new look and marketed as reflecting *new technology*. Everything has to be lumped under the heading of *new technology* because that's the only thing that sells.

You need to free yourself from the delusion that each year the new golf clubs are more forgiving and easier to play with than the clubs from the previous year. It's not true.

Forget about the hype over clubhead design and focus on the fit.

Are the irons I hit the farthest the best irons for me?

No.

When it comes to irons, most golfers think *better* means *farther*. They carry 8 to 10 irons and wedges in their bag and they try to hit each one as far as they possibly can. They may not know exactly how far they hit any club, but they definitely know it's not far enough. If they hit their 7-iron 120 yards, they definitely know they need to hit it 130 yards. If they hit their 7-iron 150 yards, they definitely know they need to hit it 160 yards.

When golfers complain to me about the distance they hit their irons, I always ask, *"If I lengthen your clubs and adjust your lofts so you'll hit each iron about 10 yards farther, can you tell me how that's going to help your game?"*

They can't, because they don't understand golf. **Irons should be designed and custom fit to maximize directional control and distance control. The key word here is *control*. Irons are control clubs. How far you hit a particular iron is irrelevant.** That's why you have so many irons in your bag. If you need to hit the ball farther, you simply select an iron with which you can hit the ball farther. That's how golf is supposed to be played.

Golfers, for some reason, don't see it that way. They believe the goal is to maximize the distance they can hit every club. They become frustrated when they only hit their 7-iron 130 yards, while their buddy hits his new 7-iron 140 yards. They feel they're playing at a disadvantage and that they need to buy new irons.

Some manufacturers understand this and are happy to give golfers what they want – irons with longer shafts and stronger lofts. They've added distance to clubs that were supposed to be designed primarily for accuracy. *That's because manufacturers are in the business of selling golf clubs, not lowering handicaps.*

So now golfers feel good about the thousand dollars they spent for their new irons, because they can hit their new 7-iron (which is really a 6-iron with a 7 stamped on it) farther than their old 7- iron. Has anything been accomplished? No. Will the golfer now score better? No.

When searching for a new set of irons, don't get wrapped up in the hottest new look. The marketing department has named the club and created the new look to sell more golf clubs, not improve your game.

How much better would I play with an expensive set of brand name irons?

Neither the cost nor brand name is relevant.

Regardless of the cost or brand name, you'll always struggle with irons that don't compliment your swing and ability. Remember, when you purchase brand name irons, you're paying for advertising, not a superior fit.

Again, you need to forget about the hype and focus on the fit.

What irons should I be using?

The irons with which you're able to produce the most controllable ball flight.

The only way to determine which irons are best for you is through being fit by a qualified club-fitter, whose fitting process is focused on *maximizing both directional and distance control.* That requires determining the clubhead design and club specifications that would allow you to make square and centered contact and achieve a playable trajectory the highest percentage of time.

This was never intended to be a *how to book* on club-fitting. I would, however, like to relate a few thoughts about iron specifications that you might want to remember.

Shaft Length

I believe most average sized golfers have at least a couple of irons in their bag that are too long.

Irons are designed to be played with a descending angle of approach (ball contact made with a slightly descending blow). Unfortunately, as the shafts get longer it becomes more difficult for the average golfer to make a good descending swing.

I've found that with clubs exceeding 38 inches in length (the length of a modern men's 5-iron), average sized male golfers generally make a better sweeping swing than descending swing. Therefore, they normally realize better results through replacing their 3 and 4-irons (and sometimes 5-iron) with either hybrid clubs or fairway metals - clubs that are designed to be played with an easier to produce sweeping swing motion.

Shaft Flex

It's a widely held belief that a stiffer shaft will provide added control and that a golfer will be wildly inconsistent with a shaft that's too flexible. Unfortunately, that belief has resulted in most golfers playing with shafts that are *too stiff.*

Generally speaking, shafts that are too stiff will negatively affect trajectory, accuracy, and feel to a greater degree than shafts that are too flexible. *When in doubt, I recommend leaning toward more flexible.*

Shaft Weight

Most golfers will generate *slightly* more clubhead speed when swinging a graphite-shafted iron. That's because graphite-shafted irons are normally *lighter* and are generally built *longer* than traditional steel-shafted irons.

Irons, however, aren't distance clubs. They're control clubs. That means you don't need a *faster* iron swing, you need a more *consistent* iron swing.

Most male golfers achieve more consistent ball striking with the slightly heavier steel-shafted irons. That's because the weight of the iron provides more feel during the swing motion. *When swinging, your body feels and responds to the weight of the club.*

Lighter graphite-shafted irons do, however, have their place. Women, juniors and seniors often achieve better results with graphite-shafted irons.

Shaft Feel

The shaft weight, flex, and bend profile will greatly affect the *feel* of the golf club during the swing motion and the *feel* of impact.

Because some golfers are *very sensitive* to feel, a clubfitter should never select a shaft strictly on the basis of computer-generated data. Before the final decision on shaft selection can be made, the club-fitter has to be assured that the golfer is comfortable with the feel of the shaft.

Playable Trajectory

The golfer should be able to achieve a *playable trajectory* with every iron they carry. That means, with every iron, the golfer should possess the ability to create a high launching trajectory that produces a descending angle steep enough that the ball will hit and stay on the green. Lower trajectories are considered *unplayable* or *unmanageable* because the golfer has no control over how far the ball will travel once it hits the green.

The truth is that most golfers are unable to *effectively* play a two, three or four-iron. Furthermore, many slower swingers are unable to *effectively* play a five or six-iron.

Again, the best option is to simply replace these irons with easier to hit hybrid clubs or high-lofted fairway metals, clubs that were specifically designed to produce a higher launch angle.

Functional Yardage Gaps

It serves no purpose to carry 2 or more irons that you hit the same, or close to the same, distance. Regardless of your ability, there should be at least a 10-yard, *playable carry distance* between each iron.

With that idea in mind, most manufacturers design their irons with a four-degree progression of lofts and a half-inch progression in lengths. In other words, the 7-iron is four-degrees stronger and a half-inch longer than the 8-iron. And the 8-iron is four-degrees stronger and a half-inch longer than the 9-iron. With the long irons the separation in loft often drops to only 3 degrees.

For most golfers, this standard progression works pretty well for their short and medium irons, but it's too narrow for their long irons. I routinely find golfers who hit their 3-iron virtually the same distance as their 4-iron, and their 4-iron only a few yards farther than their 5-iron. *This is another reason for replacing your long irons with hybrid clubs or high lofted fairway metals.*

For golfers with slower swing speeds, the standard progression between irons is too narrow across the board. These golfers would play just as well with fewer irons and wider gaps in their club-to-club specifications. Manufacturers don't offer this option because they're in the business to sell more clubs, not fewer. *And that is another reason to deal with a club maker instead of a manufacturer.*

Lie-angle

The lie-angle is the angle between the shaft and the sole of the clubhead. If you are using an iron with a *lie-angle* that fits your swing, at impact, the iron will make contact with the ground at the center of the sole. If you make contact with the ground toward the heel of the sole (in which case the toe of the iron would be pointing upward), the lie-angle of the iron would be considered too *upright* for your swing. If you make contact with the ground toward the toe of the sole (in which case you might feel the toe digging into the ground), the lie-angle of the iron would be considered too *flat* for your swing.

What golfers generally don't understand is how the lie-angle affects accuracy.

If you make *square contact* (sole line perpendicular to target line at impact) with an iron that's too upright, the face of the iron will actually be *pointed* to the left of your target. If you make *square contact* with an iron that's too flat, the face plane will actually be *pointed* to the right of the target. The greater the loft the more *mis-*

aligned the face plane becomes. This is why the lie-angle of your short irons and wedges will affect accuracy more than the lie angle of your middle and long irons.

It is also why you should have your wedges custom fit the same time you have the rest of your irons custom fit. It's the only way to insure a uniform progression of lie-angles, lofts and lengths. Too many golfers take the time to be custom fit for the 3-iron through pitching wedge, and then purchase a gap wedge, sand-iron and lob wedge off the rack. Which, from a fitting standpoint, makes no sense at all.

Grip Size & Design

It should seem obvious that a golfer with very large hands would need grips larger than a golfer with very small hands. Unfortunately, the grip size and design are normally overlooked.

The size and weight of the grip not only affects how the golf club feels in your hands, but also how your hands rotate through the hitting area. *A properly sized grip will allow you to fully control the club throughout the swing motion without tension in your hands or forearms.*

While the grip selection will ultimately be based on individual preference of feel, there are a number of factors worth considering. For example, if you like to vary the length of your iron shots through choking down on the grip, you should select a grip with less taper than standard. Otherwise, as you choke down the grip becomes too narrow, resulting in your hands gripping too tightly.

If you don't use a glove, you should select a grip specifically designed to prevent slippage. If your hands and joints are sensitive to the vibration from impact, you should consider a shock absorbing style of grip. And if you suffer from an arthritic condition in your hands, you should consider a larger grip size regardless of your hand size.

Head Design

Today, the iron head design is overrated. No manufacturer is going to try to market an unplayable iron head. From a design standpoint, if you select a mid-sized, cavity-back iron head, you can't go too far wrong. There are, however, three subtle design characteristics that you might want to consider.

Center of Gravity. Some golfers, needing a higher ball flight, have benefited *slightly* by switching to an iron head with an extremely low and rearward-positioned center of gravity. And some golfers with too high of a ball flight have acquired *slightly* better trajectory control through switching to an iron with a narrower sole and slightly higher center of gravity.

Hosel Offset. Golfers who tend to leave the clubface open at impact (heel of the clubhead leading the toe) will *sometimes* benefit by switching to a clubhead with a greater degree of hosel offset. Golfers who have trouble with the clubface being closed at impact (toe of the clubhead leading the heel) will *sometimes* benefit by switching to a clubhead with less hosel offset.

Sole Angle (Bounce). Golfers who tend to sweep the ball off the turf with no divot will often realize better results through using a clubhead design with very little bounce. Golfers with a hard descending swing motion will often take deep divots and will normally get better results by using an iron head design with added bounce.

Most golfers make the mistake of getting overly concerned with head design of their irons. The shaft, lie-angle and loft will affect impact dynamics more than the design of a *modern* iron head.

As you can see, the magic lies in the specifications of an iron, not the brand name.

Will I make more putts if I buy an expensive brand name putter?

No.

Good putting starts with the ability to correctly *read* the green. That means understanding how the condition and contour of the green along with the direction of the grain will influence a rolling golf ball.

After learning how to how to read greens (which most golfers never do), the key to good putting is distance control. And the key to distance control is a consistent quality of contact. In putting, ideal contact occurs when:

> *The ball is struck in-line with the clubhead's center of gravity (which is generally, but not always, in-line with the center of the clubface).*

> *The clubface is square (perpendicular) to the target line.*

> *The clubhead is moving down the target line and just starting its ascending arc.*

When you make ideal contact, you remove the variables that impart some degree of sidespin to the ball. The ball will come off the clubface with more of a true vertical roll. It will bounce less and, when rolling, appear to hug the ground. You'll notice this phenomenon when observing a touring professional's putt. It's referred to, among experienced golfers, as *rolling the ball*.

When you make good contact consistently, you'll acquire better distance control because distance will be dependent primarily on the single factor of clubhead speed. As your ability to control distance develops, so will your ability to judge how the ball will respond to the roll of the green. Your practice will become more productive, and you'll become a better putter.

In his book, *The Natural Way To Better Golf,* Masters and PGA champion Jackie Burke Jr. states, *"The overwhelming majority of unsuccessful putts are missed not because they were misjudged but because they were miss-hit."*

Two-time PGA champion and short game guru Paul Runyun once said, *"If there's a key to being a good putter it's having a deep understanding of how to hit the ball squarely."*

Regardless of what golf club you're using, putter, iron or driver, the story is always going to be the same. When you make contact with the ball toward the toe or heel of the clubface, the clubhead will turn, very slightly, at impact. *As a result, less energy will be transferred to the ball and the ball will travel off-line and shorter than anticipated.*

The question is would you make square and centered contact more often with an expensive brand name putter? The answer is obviously, no.

Using a putter with a head design that instills confidence and specifications that compliment your setup position and stroke, will give you the *potential* to make square and centered contact the highest percentage of time. *The cost of the putter and the brand-name will always be irrelevant.*

When you purchase a putter off the rack, you're buying a putter that was designed for an average sized golfer, who addresses the ball in the normal manner and uses what the industry considers to be a standard putting stroke. All of these putters are about 35 inches long, have a lie angle close to 72-degrees, usually a mid sized grip, and 3 or 4 degrees of loft. Regardless of how much you pay for the putter, the specs will be close to the same.

Then why are some putters so expensive?

High Moment of Inertia Putters

Some expensive putters are hyped as being *more forgiving*. These extreme perimeter-weighted putters are often referred to as *High Moment of Inertia Putters* because they'll turn *slightly less* on off-centered hits. While these putters might offer added stability, they also provide less feel. As a result, it becomes harder to determine where you're making contact on the clubface. Less feedback creates inconsistency and not one of these putters can compensate for an inconsistent stroke.

Ultimately, regardless of what putter you're using, you're not going to make many putts if you continually miss-hit the ball. No style of putter head will, in itself, solve your problems, which is why I see no value in spending a lot of money on an *extreme* perimeter-weighted putter head.

When you make consistent contact in-line with the putter head's center of gravity (which is not nearly as difficult as manufacturers would like you to believe) it doesn't matter what style of putter you use. In fact, many of the very best putters in the history of the game used a simple heel-shafted blade style of putter, which has a very low Moment of Inertia.

Alignment Style Putters

Other expensive putters are hyped as providing more accuracy. Because of their unique design, they're supposedly *easier to aim*. How much of a benefit these putters offer is also debatable. If you tossed a golf ball, underhanded, to a friend, would you need to aim your hand before you began the tossing motion? No, because your hand aligns itself to the target naturally, just as your hand will swing the clubface toward the hole naturally.

I've seen a number of successful putters (even on the PGA Tour) who don't even look at the ball or putter head. They putt by looking only at the hole. They allow their stroke to unfold naturally, just as they would if they were tossing a ball.

The truth is, many players putt exceptionally well without ever *at address* having their putter face square to their target line. It looks square to them, but it's not and it doesn't matter. *Regardless of how well you're able to align the putter face at address, the only thing that is important is the alignment of the putter face at impact.*

Designer Name Putters

Some putters are expensive because they bear the name of a popular designer and golfers see the putter being used on the PGA Tour. Most of the benefit these putters provide to the tour players came in the fitting session at the designer's studio.

Unfortunately, when you buy one of these putters, you don't get the fitting session. You do, however, get the designer's name stamped on the putter head and a cool looking putter cover. If you think that's worth a few hundred bucks, go for it.

Remember, no matter how much you pay for a putter, *you* still have to read the green and *you* still have to make the stroke.

What putter should I be using?

A putter with a head design that instills confidence, and specifications that compliment your address position and stroke.

Remember, you're *definitely* not a golf machine. You're an *individual*, with your own *individual ideas* about what you'd like your putter to look and feel like. You need to support those ideas. That's going to require that you forget about advertised hype, brand names, designer names, and who's using what putter on tour.

With that thought in mind, here are a few simple *rules of thumb* pertaining to selecting a putter.

Head Design

With regards to what putter to use, *John Jacobs* writes in his book, *50 Years of Golfing Wisdom*, *"Probably the best answer is to use the putter that gives you the best feel, or the one in which you have the most confidence. But don't stick with it if your putting goes off."*

You just need a putter with a head design that *currently* instills confidence in the address position. Only *you* will be able to determine what design that is.

The fact that you'll make the most confident stroke with the putter that you have the most confidence in is pretty obvious. Unfortunately, most golfers overlook the obvious.

Shaft length

If you play golf everyday, you can learn to putt very well with just about anything. Just take a look at the players on the PGA Tour. You'll find every style of putter, address position and putting stroke imaginable.

If you don't play golf everyday, most *experts* believe that you'll putt more consistently if you address the ball more consistently. One way to do that is to always putt with your eyes directly over the ball and parallel to the line of the putt. That's not easy to do if the length of your putter doesn't compliment your address position.

If the putter shaft is too long, you'll tend to stand too far from the ball and have to bend over significantly to get your eyes over the line of the putt. If the putter shaft is too short, you'll tend to stand too close to the ball and you'll have to stand more upright to get your eyes over the line of the putt.

You shouldn't have to adjust your stance to fit the length of the putter. *You should adjust the length of the putter to fit your stance.*

Loft

Putter loft is a specification that few golfers even think about. Even on the green, the ball tends to sit very slightly down into the grass. This is why putters are designed with a few degrees of loft. At impact, the loft will help lift the ball out of its resting position and get it rolling on line.

The question is how much loft do you need? That depends primarily on how you position your hands relative to the putter head. Most putters are designed to be played with your hands positioned only slightly ahead of the ball at impact. That design works well for most golfers because that's how most golfers putt.

If, however, you don't putt like most golfers, you would be wise to adjust the loft of your putter to better fit your individual technique. For example, if you happen to putt with your hands well ahead of the ball, you'll *deloft* the putter and possibly find that you're *bouncing* instead of *rolling* your putts. You may be able to remedy that problem through adding loft to your putter.

Conversely, if you putt with your hands slightly behind the ball you could be adding too much loft to the putter and you might develop a tendency to actually lift the ball into the air and impart added backspin to the ball. If that's the case, you might find it beneficial to reduce the loft on your putter.

> The condition of the greens is another factor to consider. If you normally putt on long, heavy greens you'll probably find it helpful to use a putter with added loft. That's because the ball will tend to sit further down into the grass.

> The opposite is true when playing very hard and fast greens. On these greens, depending on your stroke, you might get the ball rolling faster with a putter having slightly less loft.

Lie Angle

When addressing a putt, the putter head should sit flat on the ground. From this position you'll be able to better align the face plane of the putter to the target line. *You'll also scuff fewer putts.*

Grip Size

The idea is to be able to control the putter head with relaxed hands. For most golfers, that's easier to do with a larger grip.

That's all there is to it. You find a putter with a head design that instills confidence and, if needed, have the specifications altered to compliment your address position and stroke.

There's no need to spend a lot of money on a new custom-built putter. Possibly, all you'll need to do is make a few positive adjustments to the putter you're currently using. The shaft length can easily be adjusted to comfortably fit your address position and, if needed, the grip can be replaced with one that feels better in your hands. If the hosel on your putter is bendable, the lie angle and loft of the putter head can also be adjusted to better compliment your address position and stroke.

Having a properly fit putter will not alone make you a better putter. It will, however, give you the *potential* to make quality contact a higher percentage of time.

Will I hit the ball farther if I buy an expensive brand name driver?

No.

Most golfers play with a driver that's too long, too stiff and without enough loft. When they become frustrated, they spend a lot of money on a new driver that's also too long, too stiff and without enough loft.

Much has been written about the possibility of increasing your driving distance through simply replacing your current driver with the newest high-tech design. Manufacturers promote that over-sized titanium heads offer an *increased moment of inertia*, that thin titanium clubfaces provide a *higher coefficient of restitution*, and that optimizing the location of the center of gravity *positively affects the ball's launch angle and spin rate*. That all sounds important, but what does it mean? It means that marketing departments are trying to link driver performance entirely to clubhead design. That's because golfers are fascinated with clubhead design and they'll pay lots of money for it.

The greatest determinate of distance is the initial ball speed, which is determined primarily by the speed of the clubhead and quality of contact. *Golfers overestimate the importance of clubhead speed and greatly underestimate the value of square and centered contact.*

Ralph Maltby is a legendary, hall of fame, golf club designer. His book, *The Complete Golf Club Fitting Plan,* is the official fitting book used by the PGA. In the book, he states that if you miss the sweetspot of the driver face by one inch, you'll lose approximately 14% of your carry distance. Sorry, but no driver head design specification, regardless of how much you pay, can make up for that kind of distance loss. While launch angles, spin rates, moment of inertia and coefficient of restitution might be interesting stuff (to somebody), if your primary concern is increasing the distance of your average drive, your primary goal should be to select a driver that allows you to make square and centered contact the highest percentage of time.

In his book, *Golf Begins at Forty,* Sam Snead was referring to the value of square and centered contact when he wrote *"You will hit the ball farther more frequently when you don't try to hit it far."*

Jack Nicklaus was also referring to the value of square and centered contact when he wrote in his book, *My Story, "There are really two ways to increase your distance. You can learn to swing the clubhead faster. Or you can learn to deliver it to the ball more accurately."*

Marketing departments don't emphasize the value of square and centered contact because golfers don't get excited about square and centered contact. (In other words, it's a good idea but it doesn't sell drivers.) Golfers get excited about clubhead design, but no clubhead design can provide a higher percentage of center hits.

While manufacturers would love for you to believe that you'll always hit the more expensive driver farther, it's obviously not true. The driver you'll hit consistently farther is the one that best compliments your swing and ability. As always, you need to be concerned with the specifications, not the brand name.

What driver should I be using?

The driver with which you are able to make square and centered contact, with an acceptable trajectory, the highest percentage of time.

Most golfers get fit for a driver as though they were entering a long drive contest. Have you ever seen a long drive contest? Each contestant is judged on his or her best of three drives. If two of their drives miss the fairway by 100 yards it doesn't matter. Unfortunately, that's not how golf is played. You only get to hit your drive once and then you have to go find it. That's why, if you want to play golf well, you better use a driver with which you're able to make square and centered contact a high percentage of time.

Your ability to select that driver is dependent primarily on how well you can answer the following three fundamental questions:

#1 *What driver SHAFT will provide CENTERED CONTACT the highest percentage of time?*

Regardless of how much money you spent on the *high tech* design of the clubhead, to achieve maximum distance, you're still going to have to make contact in the center of the clubface. Unfortunately, even a $500 clubhead can't deliver itself to the ball. *It's the job of the shaft to deliver the clubhead to the ball.*

Your first priority should always be to select a shaft that will allow *you* to make *centered contact* the highest percentage of time. Determining what shaft that would be is accomplished through a process of trial and error.

For most of my life, I (and just about every other male golfer) played with a 43" steel-shafted driver. When high-quality graphite shafts emerged in the 1990's, most of us switched to a much longer graphite shafted driver with an oversized titanium head. Today, I still play with a titanium driver head, but I dropped the extra long graphite shaft years ago.

The long lightweight graphite shaft and over-sized titanium head appeared to be a great match. In theory, the longer and lighter shaft would provide added clubhead speed and the larger head would be more forgiving on off-center hits. *Unfortunately, the extra long shaft produced a higher percentage of miss-hits than anticipated and the large titanium head was not nearly as forgiving as it was advertised to be.*

Today, for some reason, most golfers are still playing with a driver shaft that's too long. For that reason, they don't make centered contact nearly as often as they could.

#2 *What FACE ANGLE will provide SQUARE CONTACT the highest percentage of time?*

Making contact in the center of the clubface is one thing, making contact with a square clubface is another. Golfers often confuse the two. While a number of design factors will influence your ability to square the clubface, the most dominant factor is the *face angle* of the clubhead.

If you consistently make contact with the clubface either open or closed to the intended target line, the easiest way to correct that tendency is through using a driver with a compensating *face angle*. Again, that determination can only be made through trial and error and only after selecting the appropriate shaft.

You can observe your driver's face angle, after taking your address position, by allowing the driver head to sit flat on the ground. For a right-handed golfer, if the face angle is *closed*, the face of the driver will be aiming to the left of the target line. If the face angle is *open*, the face of the driver will be aiming to the right of the target line.

Because most golfers have a tendency to make contact with the face slightly open, using a driver head with *slightly closed face angle* helps them square the clubface at impact a higher percentage of time.

#3 What driver LOFT will provide an ACCEPTABLE LAUNCH ANGLE the highest percentage of time?

Before you can determine an optimal launch angle for your driver, you need to consider your normal playing conditions. As a general rule of thumb, it's best to select a loft that will maximize the carry distance of the driver. That, however, is only a general rule of thumb. If you normally play in windy conditions or on very hard fairways, you will benefit from a slightly lower launch angle.

If your goal is to maximize carry distance, determining the optimal launch angle is a matter of simple physics. It's dependent on clubhead speed. *The slower the clubhead speed, the higher the ball will have to be launched.*

You cannot, however, select an appropriate driver loft entirely on the basis of clubhead speed. You must also consider your *angle of approach* (the angle in which *you* normally bring the clubhead to the ball). If you normally make contact with the driver head traveling on the upswing (*positive angle of approach*), you'll normally add loft to your driver. If you normally make contact with the driver head traveling downward (*negative angle of approach*), you'll actually be taking loft off the driver.

The *effective loft* (loft at impact) is therefore determined by both the loft of the driver and the clubhead's angle of approach. What this means is that the driver loft that will produce an optimal launch angle for *you*, once again, can only be determined through trial and error.

If you can't answer the above three fundamental questions (which very few golfers can), and if you're not going to take the time to be properly fit (which very few golfers do), why would you think you're going to hit an expensive brand name driver any better than your old driver?

Are launch monitors just more hype?

Yes and no.

When metal drivers were first introduced, an interesting thing happened. Manufacturers started offering drivers in a variety of lofts. In the past this was not the case. The driver was simply identified as the number one wood, and most golfers didn't give the actual loft of the driver much consideration. Suddenly, we had to determine if we were playing the driver with the correct loft. Most of us figured (incorrectly) that we could hit the ball farther with less loft, so that's the direction we took. Soon we were all hitting low line drives off the tee and trying to convince ourselves that we were actually hitting the ball farther.

As time passed and more information surfaced, driver loft evolved into quite an issue. Equipment gurus determined that golfers should strive to increase their driver carry distance, not rolling distance. For most golfers, that would require using a driver with more loft. Unfortunately, that's not an easy sell. It just didn't seem right that a golfer could drive the ball farther with a twelve-degree driver than he could with a seven-degree driver. Besides, we had become so used to seeing low line drives, a proper trajectory appeared to be way too high.

While the debate over trajectory was carrying on, there was also a lot being written about ball spin rates. Testing revealed that the driver carry distance would be reduced with either too much or too little ball spin. In extreme cases, golfers could actually see how vertical spin was influencing the flight of the golf ball. With the ideal amount of spin, the ball would peak and appear to hold that trajectory before slowly drifting downward. With too little spin, the ball would appear to peak and then quickly drop out of the air. With too much spin, the ball would peak and then appear to spin upward before dropping out of the air.

While all of this sounded interesting, it was also confusing. How could a golfer select a driver that would provide the ideal launch angle and spin rate?

Soon, many clubfitters started using *launch monitors* to eliminate the confusion. Better launch monitors could measure a golf ball's initial speed, trajectory and spin rate.

In theory, once the initial ball speed is known, the fitter could check his charts and determine what launch angle and spin rate would maximize the ball's carry distance.

Basic physics.

Then the fitter would have the golfer hit a variety of drivers and balls on the launch monitor to determine which combination provided the target launch angle and spin rate. No more guesswork. The launch monitor would supply all the data needed.

For a while, there was a lot of excitement about launch angles and spin rates. Unfortunately, in the end, it was just another theory that, for the average golfer, was more hype than substance. *Even if you were able to purchase the perfect driver, you must remember that it's only going to work perfectly when you're able to apply the clubhead to the ball perfectly.* Good Luck.

After you've purchased your *perfectly fit* $500 driver, here are a few of the factors that will influence your *perfect* launch angle and *ideal* spin rate the 95% of the time that you don't make a perfect swing,

> 1) If you make contact with the clubhead traveling down the target line, but the face angle is slightly closed (toe leading heel), you'll decrease the launch angle and impart sidespin (hook spin) onto the ball.

> 2) If you make contact with the clubhead traveling down the target line, but the face angle is slightly open (heel leading toe), you'll increase the launch angle and impart sidespin (slice spin) onto the ball.

3) If you make contact with the ball high on the clubface, you'll increase the launch angle (due to the roll of the face) and reduce the spin rate (due to the vertical gear effect).

4) If you make contact with the ball low on the clubface, you'll decrease the launch angle (due to the roll of the face) and increase the spin rate (due to the vertical gear effect).

5) If you make contact with the ball more on the upswing than normal (a more *positive* angle of approach) you'll increase the launch angle and decrease the spin rate.

6) If you make contact with the ball more on the downswing than normal (a more *negative* angle of approach) you'll decrease the launch angle and increase the spin rate.

The fact is that anytime you make contact anywhere on the clubface other than the point in-line with the clubhead's center of gravity, the clubhead will turn at impact. This will reduce the speed in which the ball leaves the clubface and influence the spin rate.

Oh well.

Certainly launch monitors have their place, but only when working with the very best golfers; those golfers who make square and centered contact, with a consistent angle of approach, a very high percentage of time. These very talented players can realize a measurable increase in distance through the *synergetic effect* of using an optimal head design (in terms of center of gravity location), an optimal ball design (in terms of spin rate) and an optimal loft (that perfectly compliments their very consistent angle of approach and clubhead speed).

The rest of us have a hard enough time just getting the clubface on the ball. For us, the objective should be to select a driver that will provide the highest percentage of square and centered hits and an *acceptable* average trajectory.

Also, when you hear a PGA Tour player speak of the success they've had through working with a launch monitor, don't equate their success with the experience you're going to have at the local discount center. Tour players work with the finest equipment and highly experienced technicians. You, on the other hand, will probably find yourself hitting into a net and working with an unqualified salesperson trying to interpret data from poorly calibrated equipment.

Obviously, you would be far better off on an outdoor driving range, working with a qualified clubfitter. Sure, there are clubfitters who are going to swear that the information generated from their $5000 launch monitor will greatly benefit all golfers. That's because these fitters are trying to justify their $5000 investment.

When we spend too much time on launch angles and spin rates, all we do is take our focus away from the much more critical issue of square and centered contact.

Does it really matter if I get fit inside or outside?

Do you want to get fit by numbers or ball flight?

Getting fit for golf clubs while hitting into a net is always going to be a gamble, because you can't see the ball flight. You have to rely on the salespersons ability to correctly interpret *questionable* computer generated data. I refer to the process as *fitting by numbers*. Sometimes it works okay (mostly by luck) and sometimes it's a disaster.

Salespersons like it because there's no *thinking* involved. They don't have to answer many questions because the customer can't see where the ball is going. The numbers tell the entire story and the customer is led to believe that the numbers are always right.

When you get fit outside, on a driving range, *ball-flight* tells the story. There's no gamble involved. No smoke and mirrors. You don't need a salesperson to tell you how you're hitting the ball because it's obvious. You know immediately if you can hit the ball better with the new clubs or not.

What's the most important aspect of clubfitting?

For the average golfer, it's set composition.

Once an elderly golfer stopped by my shop to show me his new *custom fit* set of brand name irons. The irons were quite expensive, but he felt good about the price because the fitting process had been so thorough. My concern was with the set composition. Because I was familiar with his golfing ability, I knew that he would be unable to achieve a *playable trajectory with* either the 3,4 or 5-iron, regardless of how well *fit* they were. Carrying clubs you can't hit serves no purpose. These clubs should have been replaced with either hybrid clubs or fairway metals.

I don't know how you can be properly fit for golf clubs you can't hit, but it happens all the time. Especially at large discount golf centers. Buyers routinely end up with at least one club (and sometimes three or four clubs) they don't have the ability to effectively use.

You're only allowed to carry fourteen clubs when you play golf, but you get to pick any fourteen clubs you want. You need to open your mind and figure out which fourteen clubs work best for *you*. I've seen players on the PGA Tour carry five wedges and I've seen players on the PGA Tour play with only two wedges. I've seen professionals play with five fairway metals and I've seen professionals play with a driver, putter and twelve irons. Many touring professionals have replaced a number of their irons or fairway metals with hybrid clubs. Phil Mickelson won The Masters with two drivers. Other players have had success with two putters.

The best players in the world have no problem altering their set composition and neither should you. You should be able to *effectively* use every club in your bag and every club should have a *specific purpose.*

When dealing with the average golfer, I consider formulating the set composition to be the most important aspect of the fitting process. Retailers, however, like to overlook set composition because selling a full set of irons is an easy sell. Also, selling the standard set composition is much easier for a poorly trained fitter. *It requires no thinking.*

How do most manufacturers and retailers deal with custom club fitting?

They keep the process as simple as possible.

To do a proper job, a clubfitter needs to have a good understanding of the golf swing, the manufacturer's equipment, and modern fitting procedures. That means people have to be trained and retail outlets have to create fitting areas.

The manufacturers who have embarked on training programs have found the process to be expensive, frustrating and never ending. Golf professionals often have their own (often antiquated) ideas about fitting and changing their minds is usually difficult and sometimes impossible. Salespeople, on the other hand, change jobs on a regular basis and need to be trained continually.

For the manufacturer, selling custom fit golf clubs means dealing with incompetent fitters, confusing custom orders, and handling an increased number of mistakes. For retailers it means continually repairing and updating fitting equipment and continually training new salespersons.

Trust me, manufacturers and retailers would both love to scrap the whole idea of custom fitting and return to the *easy money days* of just selling pre-assembled golf clubs off a rack. Fortunately, they can't do that because custom fitting has become a service that many buyers expect.

So what they do is ease the pain by keeping the fitting process as simple as possible. They view it more as a *sales tool* than a benefit to the golfer. *Which is another reason for dealing with an independent clubmaker.*

How much would a properly fit set of golf clubs really help me?

It's an important step, but only one step to becoming a better golfer.

The goal of the clubfitter is to provide you with a set of golf clubs that will give you the *potential* to make square and centered contact, with a playable trajectory, the highest percentage of time. Clubs that will give you the *potential* to acquire better distance control.

There is, however, something you need to understand. If your shot selection remains poor, if you continually choose to address the ball in a haphazard manner, and allow your mind to wander while you're swinging, new golf clubs are not going to solve your problems. **Better tools are no value to someone who doesn't know how to use them.**

Acquiring a properly fit set of golf clubs is an important step, but only *one step* toward becoming a better golfer. *If you want to score lower, you're going to have to learn how to play golf better.*

A few points to remember about your golf clubs

Whenever you find yourself being lured in by the high-tech hype of the golf club industry, before you pull out your credit card, remember these points...

- **Don't be misled into believing a golf club is more than just a golf club.**

- **Regardless of what you might hear from manufacturers, today the magic lies more in *golf club fitting* than in *high-tech design*.**

- **Brand name golf clubs will always be expensive because you're paying for advertising.**

- **As far as the average golfer is concerned, everything that can be done to significantly improve the performance of a golf club has already been done.**

- **To produce a legal golf club, manufacturers have to stay within the guidelines set forth by the ruling bodies of golf. So if you've been waiting for some future advance in golf club design to dramatically improve the quality of your game, you can forget about it.**

- **Just because golf clubs look different every year doesn't mean they're getting better. If they didn't look different you wouldn't keep buying them.**

- A better golf club is one with which you have the *potential* to make square and centered contact and achieve a playable trajectory a higher percentage of time. You'll seldom be lucky enough to find that club on a shelf. It can, however, be acquired through working with a qualified clubfitter.

- Golf clubs are market driven, not performance driven. Which means manufacturers are more interested in selling golf clubs than lowering handicaps.

- Modern mechanical swing machines can generate results that will make any clubhead appear to be far more than it is.

- The modern equipment is not the primary reason today's professional golfers hit the ball farther and score lower. Advances in technology have, without question, had an impact on the game. The degree of impact, however, has been grossly exaggerated in an effort to sell golf clubs.

- Advances in equipment design have not helped the average golfer score better. Today's golfer is scoring no better than the average golfer did 30 years ago.

- You need to free yourself from the delusion that each year the new golf clubs are more forgiving and easier to play with than the clubs from the previous year. It's not true.

- When purchasing golf clubs, your primary concern should always be related to the fit. Forget about the hype over brand names, clubhead cosmetics, and who is playing what equipment on tour.

- When you purchase brand name golf clubs, you're paying for advertising, not a superior fit.

- Irons are control clubs, not distance clubs. You don't need irons that hit the ball farther, you need irons that provide better directional and distance control.

- Regardless of how much you pay for a putter, you're still going to be the one reading the green and you're still going to be the one making the stroke. All you need is a putter with a head design that instills confidence and specifications that fit your setup position and stroke.

- Becoming overly concerned with launch angles and spin rates, takes your focus away from the much more critical issue of square and centered contact.

- When you hear a PGA Tour player speak of the success they've had through working with a launch monitor, don't equate their success with the experience you're going to have at the local discount center. Tour players work with the finest equipment and highly experienced technicians. You will probably find yourself hitting into a net and working with an unqualified salesperson trying to interpret data from poorly calibrated equipment.

- Giant golf club manufacturers and retailers deal with custom club fitting through keeping the fitting process as simple as possible. They treat it more as a sales tool than a benefit to the golfer.

- It's far better to be fit by *ball flight* (outside) than *numbers* (inside).

- For the average golfer, determining the correct *set composition* is the most important aspect of clubfitting.

- Acquiring a properly fit set of golf clubs will give you the *potential* to improve your ball-striking and lower your average score. That potential, however, will be limited to your understanding of the game.

PART TWO

QUESTIONS
you should be asking about
YOUR GOLF SWING

You must have worked very hard to get this bad.

- Ernest Jones
  Legendary Swing Instructor
  Speaking to a student

*Golf is assuredly a mystifying game. It would seem that if a person
has hit a golf ball correctly a thousand times, he should be able to
duplicate the performance at will. But this is certainly not the case.*

- Bobby Jones

Does it really matter how I swing?

No.

Who was the best ball-striker of all time? When I was younger, that was a question I loved to ask. I figured that if I could identify the best ball striker, I could study his swing mechanics and I might discover his *secret*. Like most golfers, I believed great ball striking was a product of great swing mechanics.

Unfortunately, even the most respected golf historians don't entirely agree on who the best ball-striker of all time was. While all the experts had their own opinion, three names seemed to always come up, Ben Hogan, Lee Trevino and Moe Norman. Three self-taught players with three distinctively different swings and three distinctively different ideas about how to hit a golf ball!

They didn't share some swing secret, because there was no secret. That's because, as I eventually learned, it doesn't matter how you swing. *What set these great players apart was their approach to the game, not their swing.* They were loners, and they were very comfortable *not* following the crowd. They had no interest in studying current swing theories, because they had no interest in trying to look like someone else. They shared one objective - to hit the ball straighter than anyone else. It didn't matter how they did it, it didn't matter what they looked liked, and they weren't concerned with the opinion of others. Their reasoning was something along the lines of, *why would I want to swing like someone else if my intention is to hit the ball straighter than everyone else?*

Today is the era of computer enhanced video analysis and golf swing gurus. With all the advances in swing instruction, how many current players strike the ball better than Hogan, Trevino or Norman? None. Why?

Well there's one thing that I do know. Unlike Trevino, Hogan and Norman, today's players tend to give a great deal of credence to the opinion of others. **Trying to adjust your body position during the swing motion, in an effort to perfectly emulate someone else's golf swing, or someone else's idea of what your golf swing should look like, has proven not to be the optimal way to improve your ball striking.**

In his classic work *The Art of Golf,* Sir Walter Simpson wrote, *"Copying the style of a champion is as profitless as copying Hamlet in the hopes of becoming a Shakespeare."*

Still, it's a widely held belief that a *better* golf swing automatically creates *better* ball striking. Many very good players have actually spent their entire careers trying to improve their ball-striking through developing a *better* golf swing. What constitutes a *better* golf swing anyway?

Legendary golf instructor John Jacobs states, *"The only object of the golf swing is to present the club correctly to the ball."* If you look at the swings of the top players in the world, you'll find that each player uses a different method to *present the club correctly to the ball.*

The fact that the top 100 players in the world all have different swings, should tell you something. It should tell you that how you swing is not nearly as important as you've been led to believe. It seems illogical that there are so many ways to successfully swing a golf club. Yet, it's true. As John Jacobs further states, *"One reason I have always thought that golf can be such a difficult game is that there are so many ways to play it correctly."*

That's a quote all golfers (and swing instructors) should remember.

Is there a best way to swing?

Yes, the way that works best for you.

After accepting that it really doesn't matter how you swing, the next question is always the same – *which way is best?*

What's the *correct* way to chip? What's the *proper* way to hit sand shots? What's the *best* way to swing a golf club? These are questions I hear around the golf course all the time.

As a rule, golf professionals tend to view the simpler method as being the *better* method. They normally prefer the swing that has fewer moving parts and fewer idiosyncrasies. While such a swing might *appear* to be easier to control, that's all you can say about it. There is certainly no guarantee that a golfer with a simpler swing will strike the ball consistently better than a golfer with an unorthodox swing. As Masters, PGA, and United States Open champion, Raymond Floyd once said, *"If a great golf swing put you high on the money list, many of us would be broke."*

Despite what you might hear from the golf industry, there is no *one* best *way* to do anything. There is only the way that works best for you. To determine what method that is, you have two choices. You can follow the footsteps of Hogan, Trevino and Norman, and spend most of your life on a driving range (Hogan referred to this route as *digging the answer out of the dirt*). Or you can save a lot of time and find yourself a good golf coach.

I refer to a *golf coach* as someone who will help you find the swing that works best for you. Unfortunately, most golf instructors don't take this approach. Instead they teach their own preconceived ideas on how everyone should swing a golf club. They generally adhere to the notion that there is indeed a *best way* to do everything – their way.

When following the advice of a swing instructor, the student often gets so involved with learning a particular method of swinging, they forget how to play golf. They become convinced that they have to stick with the swing they've been taught because it's the *correct way* to swing. If they fail to improve, they believe that it's due to a lack of practice or talent. Actually, that's rarely the case. **They generally fail to improve because they're approaching golf in a manner that just doesn't work for them.**

In his book, *My Story*, Jack Nicklaus writes about the philosophy of his life long instructor Jack Grout, *"Jack always wanted you to do it 'your way', the most natural way you could, which made him the polar opposite of all those pros who want you to do it their way, or to adopt some 'method' they believe they've invented for the salvation of golfers everywhere."*

Just as you are an individual, so should your swing be.

Can I ever learn to swing the same way twice?

No.

I spent my early years in golf committed to the goal of building a *repeating swing*. Through my high school and college years, the *repeating swing* was the hot topic. We were all trying to develop a *big muscle swing* that was easy to repeat and that would never *breakdown* under pressure. Ben Hogan was my hero, and his 1957 book, *Five Lessons: The Modern Fundamentals of Golf,* was my golf Bible. I memorized the 127-page book and I kept a copy in my bag at all times.

Hogan wrote, *"It is utterly impossible for any golfer to play good golf without a swing that will repeat"*; and I took it to heart. It seems the golf industry took it to heart as well. For years, everything I read was based on the assumption that success in golf was predicated on developing a *repeating swing*.

Then one day I read Michael Murphy's book, *Golf in the Kingdom*. I enjoyed the book and remember chuckling to myself when Shivas Irons, the central figure – a mystically gifted golf professional – told his playing partners that he never used the same swing twice. I remember thinking how absurd it would be for a great player to make such a ridiculous statement.

Today I laugh when I think about the years I spent in the useless pursuit of a *repeating* golf swing. There are an endless number of factors that will determine how you will swing a golf club at any particular time. *While your mindset will obviously have the greatest influence,* your physical condition, flexibility, energy level, address position, alignment, and even the weather will all affect your swing as well.

Since all these factors are interrelated and constantly changing, it's unlikely that you'll ever swing a golf club *exactly* the same way twice. Unfortunately, most golfers have become preoccupied with trying to swing their golf club *exactly* the same way every time. When they can't, they complain about how frustrating golf is.

It's time to clear your mind and forget all the hype about a repeating golf swing. You'll never have one and you don't need one. **Golf is not about static conditions and perfect mechanical repetition. It's about changing circumstances and your ability to adapt to those circumstances.** When golfers center their attention on trying to develop a repeating swing, too much emphasis is given to swing mechanics. Trying to play golf through focusing on technique just doesn't work.

In his book, *Bobby Jones on Golf,* Jones writes, *"A few disasters resulting from a desire to display brilliant technique are enough to harden even the most sensitive nature.... Once the round is under way, the business at hand becomes that of getting results. Nothing else matters."*

Why does my golf swing keep changing?

Primarily because you allow your alignment and setup position to keep changing.

After spending a few years trying to develop a repeating golf swing, most golfers will eventually give up. They'll conclude that their swing will always be changing and that there's not much they can do about it. While it's true that they'll never have a perfectly repeating golf swing, they can certainly learn how to keep their swing under better control.

Have you ever noticed how much attention professionals give to their alignment and setup position? Peter Thompson, the legendary Australian golfer who won five British opens, said that everything you needed to know about golf swing technique could be written on two sheets of paper, and that 90 percent of it would deal with *getting set up right*.

Jack Nicklaus, in his classic book *Golf My Way*, wrote that hitting a good golf shot was fifty percent mental picture, forty percent setup, and only ten percent swing. In other words, he felt that ninety percent of what it takes to hit a good golf shot (make a good golf swing) happened *before the swing even began*.

Golfers don't appreciate the importance of their setup position because they don't take the time to understand how the various aspects of their setup position directly influence their swing motion and the quality of ball contact. Golfers need to always remember that:

How they position their hips, legs and feet will affect their balance and ability to turn in both directions.

How they align their shoulders and distribute their weight will greatly influence the path of the clubhead.

How they position the ball in their stance will affect the clubhead's angle of approach and the alignment of the clubface at impact.

How they grip the club will affect how the clubface will rotate through the impact area.

Your swing motion is *guided by* and *moves around* your setup position. If your setup position changes, your swing motion will change. It has to change. To achieve a more consistent swing motion, *you must* learn to address the ball and align yourself in a more consistent manner. The best players know that this is much easier said than done. And that's why they work at it continuously.

While golfers wonder why their swing motion keeps changing, they should be wondering why their alignment and setup position keep changing.

Why does my alignment and setup position keep changing?

Fear and a subconscious effort to get it right.

We learn all physical skills through a natural subconscious process. **Through a series of failures, each followed by a subconscious correction, we keep getting a little better at something until we eventually *get it right*.** It's how we learn to do everything from riding a bike to hitting a golf ball.

While we never forget how to ride a bike, it *seems* like we routinely forget how to hit a golf ball. And every time we miss-hit a shot our body returns to the process of making the corrections it feels are necessary to once again *get it right*.

We also *naturally* and *subconsciously* move away from what we fear. On the golf course, the subconscious process of *moving away from our fears* and *adjusting to our mistakes* is easily observable. For example, right-handed golfers who habitually hook the ball will inevitably (and unknowingly) start aligning themselves to the right of their target. They'll sense that they're aimed directly at the target, but their perception will be distorted by the *fear* of missing shots to the left. For the same reason, right-handed golfers who habitually slice the ball will inevitably (and unknowingly) start aiming to the left of their target.

As these golfers allow their alignment to change, they'll notice the emergence of a more sporadic shot pattern. That will trigger subconscious adjustments to other aspects of their setup position, normally their grip and ball position. In one way or another, your body will always try to *learn from and respond to the previous shot.* Which is why you can never take your alignment or setup position for granted.

So if our body is always changing in an effort to *get it right*, how come it doesn't eventually *get it right*? How come we never forget how to ride a bike, but we routinely forget how to hit a golf ball?

Actually, we never *forget* how to do anything. We just allow our *conscious* thoughts to interfere with our natural *subconscious* ability. When hitting a golf ball, instead of allowing our body to move as a natural *effortless* response to our intention, we feel the need to control it. But, because our swing moves faster then we can think, attempts to consciously control it don't work. In fact, they do nothing more than throw the swing off balance.

If every time you rode a bike you tried to control every movement of your body, I guarantee that you'd throw yourself off balance and fall down a lot more often. Then you'd wonder why you *keep forgetting* how to ride a bike.

In preparing to ride a bike, you *consciously* balance and align the bike before you mount it. Then you allow your natural *subconscious* ability to keep you in balance as you ride. **Similarly, in golf, you should *consciously* align yourself and assume the correct setup position. Then you allow your natural *subconscious* ability to swing the golf club.**

Why is it that sometimes I set up good and still swing bad?

You're a human swing machine, not a mechanical swing machine.

There is something you need to remember about your golf swing – *it doesn't exist apart from you.* While that statement would seem obvious to anyone, to golfers it's not.

As golfers, we normally refer to our golf swing as though it was our second car. We're always *working* on it. We enjoy analyzing the various parts, trying to *fix* this or eliminate that.

We also love to diagnose our miss-hits in mechanical terms. We say that we *looked up*, that we *swung too fast*, or that we *swayed on the backswing*. When we play really bad, we say that our swing has completely *broken down*. When our car breaks down we take it to a mechanic, when our swing breaks down we take it to golf professional.

The point is, that at some level, we start perceiving our golf swing as though it existed apart from our body. As though it were something that another person could fix or adjust when it goes out of form. We have this strange idea that our golf swing should be able to work properly, regardless of our fears, intention or ability to focus. If we line it up correctly, it's supposed to work.

Dealing with your swing *motion*, however, is very different than dealing with either your setup position or alignment. Once you've setup to the ball and made your takeaway, the balance of your golf swing moves too fast to be successfully controlled. You can, to a degree, control the tempo, but not the myriad of movements that compose the motion.

Your swing motion reflects your *current* perception of how to hit a golf ball coupled with your *current* physical condition and – most importantly – *state of mind*. The problem lies primarily in the fact that the swing motion is influenced by a conscious awareness that's bombarded by an incessant stream of random thoughts and sensory stimuli. *In other words, an awareness that's constantly changing.*

The next time you hit a poor golf shot, instead of trying to determine the mechanical flaw, try to remember what you were thinking. Have you ever noticed how fluid and effortless your swing motion is when you're well rested, relaxed, and carefree? How balanced it is when your not overly concerned with the *results*?

Have you ever noticed how inconsistent your swing is when you're fatigued, nervous, or unable to hold a *clear intention*? When you try to hit the golf ball through trying to consciously control some body movement, have you noticed how disjointed and out of rhythm your swing becomes?

To understand your swing motion, you don't need to take a video of it. What's happening on the outside is only a *reflection* of what's happening on the inside. As golf writer Lorne Rubenstein states, *"Hitting a golf ball is an act so precise that there is unlimited room for error. That error begins in the mind and finds expression in the swing."*

Golfers, unfortunately, are so obsessed with trying to fix the reflection (their swing), they give little thought to what's causing it (their thinking).

If my swing moves too fast to be consciously controlled, how do I control it?

Through focusing on what you can control.

You can't *directly* control your swing motion, because it moves faster than you can think. You can only control it *indirectly*. That's done through giving your attention *exclusively* to the four things that you can control – *how you setup to the ball, your intention, how you initiate your swing, and the tempo of your swing*. When you consider the *cause and effect* nature of the golf swing, the importance of these four factors becomes obvious. Let me explain.

How you setup to the ball and align yourself

Your swing is *guided by* and *moves around* your setup position. It's the foundation of your swing and you should make a conscious effort to ensure that it *always* compliments your intention. *Why almost all golfers take their setup position and alignment for granted, I have no idea.*

Your intention

Your swing motion, to a great degree, reflects your intention. For example, the intention to *hit the ball hard* will often result in a

71

quick and off-balanced motion that produces poor contact. The intention to *stay down* often results in an incomplete backswing, an overly steep downswing, and the clubhead making contact with the ground before the ball.

Since the successful outcome of almost every shot will be dependent on your ability to make square and centered contact, that should always be your intention - *to make square and centered contact.*

How you initiate your swing

Exactly how you set the various parts of your body in motion will greatly influence both the tempo and balance of your entire swing. Jack Nicklaus writes, *"The most important single move in establishing your tempo and rhythm is your takeaway. It sets the beat for everything that comes later."*

If you initiate your swing in a balanced and properly paced manner, it will tend to unfold in a balanced and properly faced manner. On the other hand, if you initiate your swing motion in an *off-tempo* or *out-of-balance* manner, it will only have about one second to *correct itself* before contact.

Does that tell you something? *It should tell you that how you initiate your swing might be worth thinking about.*

The tempo of your swing.

If you start the swing in balance, your natural tempo will *keep* the swing in balance.

Five time major champion, Nick Faldo states, *"Whether you hit the ball slowly, soft, or hard, everyone needs tempo...Tempo is the glue that sticks all elements of the golf swing together."*

Your body *turns back and forth*, your arms *swing up and down*, and your wrists *cock upward and then release*. To make a good swing, these movements have to occur in balance. That's easiest done when you swing at your natural tempo.

So that's how you control your *uncontrollable* swing motion. You give your attention exclusively to what you can control *–how you setup to the ball, your intention, how you initiate your swing and the tempo of your swing.*

It's simply a matter of cause and effect.

How do I start my swing?

With as little effort as possible.

The swing motion should obviously be seamless. As the legendary golf instructor Ernest Jones wrote, "You can't divide the swing into parts and still have a swing." But when golfers are told exactly how they should consciously control their takeaway, they start to wonder about other phases of their swing. They start to perceive the swing motion as a series of *consciously controllable* movements and positions.

This is why many golf coaches never use the term *takeaway*. They feel that the term itself implies conscious manipulation. Instead, they prefer subjective terms like *moveaway* or *swingaway*. Jack Nicklaus tried to address the issue when he wrote, *"Strive on every shot to move the club back as deliberately as possible, consistent with 'swinging it' rather than 'taking it'.* In other words, do it correctly but without *trying*.

When you *try* to control the first part of your swing it becomes difficult to allow the balance of the swing to unfold freely. That's why you should initiate your swing motion with as little effort as possible. Through allowing the swing to *start on its own*, you can take conscious manipulation out of the equation from the very beginning.

Many golfers have had success using use some type of *trigger* to start their swing motion; an unrelated movement that would *signal* the body to start the swing. Nicklaus would turn his head, Player would kick-in his right knee, Bobby Jones would turn his left hip backward, and Tom kite would bounce on his knees. Many players have had success using either a forward press or a waggle as a trigger. The idea is to get the swing moving *on its own;* to keep the process as natural as possible.

How do I swing without tension and effort?

Swing without thought.

Without thought, tension and effort disappear and your swing returns to being a natural *effortless* response to your intention.

Ben Crenshaw wrote, *"Once I've started the putter in motion, it's as if it's swinging itself."* That's how you should perceive your full swing motion. With no controlling thoughts, you merely hold the intention of making square and centered contact and *allow* your swing to unfold as spontaneously and naturally as possible.

The practice of doing something without conscious effort is referred to in Taoism as *wu-wei*. In Eastern philosophy, it is considered to be the most efficient way to do anything. Action that is done with a mind free of thought and self consciousness is considered *supreme action*.

In the West, however, we tend to view the practice of doing something without conscious effort to be lazy and ineffectual. That perspective is quite apparent in the way we approach golf. We over analyze, manipulate and force.

Philosopher Alan Watts was a renowned interpreter of Zen Buddhism for the West. He once said, *"Really, the best meaning of wu-wei is 'don't force it'... This is like sailing a boat. It is more intelligent to sail a boat that to row it, even though sailing is a lazier way of doing it."*

The best way to swing a golf club will always be without thought. To sail, instead of row!

Would acquiring a detailed mechanical understanding of the golf swing help me swing better?

No.

When you try to understand the golf swing from the standpoint of mathematics and physics, it becomes ridiculously confusing. Fortunately, you can play great golf without ever having to define your swing in terms of angular momentum, centrifugal acceleration, and geometric planes. In fact, it seems that the more you try to apply science to golf, the more you misunderstand the game. As the great Bobby Jones put it, *"Anyone who hopes to reduce putting – or any other department of the game of golf for that matter – to an exact science, is in for a serious disappointment, and will only suffer from the attempt."*

Have you ever wondered why the best teachers aren't the best players? It's because becoming a student of the golf swing is one thing and becoming a good golfer is another.

If your goal is to become a good golfer, all you need is a *general understanding* of swing mechanics. You need to know just enough to keep your rational mind satisfied and quiet. When you hit a poor shot, your rational mind needs to understand what physically happened. You weren't trying to hit a poor shot, so it needs a satisfying explanation. Information it can use to make *what it believes to be* the appropriate corrections. Without these *corrections*, you'll play with the fear that the same mistake could, at any time, occur again.

The golf swing is difficult to understand because it's composed of different parts of the body moving in different directions, at different speeds and on different planes. It becomes much easier to consider when it's broken down into four basic components, the *setup position* and three movements: *the turn* of the body, *the swing* of the arms, and *the cocking* of the wrists.

When the setup position is correct and each movement occurs *in balance* with the other two, you create a good golf swing. When the setup position is incorrect, or when one of the three movements is *out of balance* your entire swing will be *out of balance.*

Acquiring a *general* understanding of how each of these four basic components work together is all you'll ever need to know. With that knowledge, you'll be able to clearly explain the fundamental golf swing and the mechanical reason for every miss-hit. *As far as your golf game is concerned, there is no reason to delve any further into the study of swing mechanics.*

I like the quote I recently read from sports psychologist Dr. Fran Pirozollo, *"A physicist can describe the perfect golf swing and write it down in scientific language, but the smart golfer doesn't read it. The smart golfer gives it to his opponent to contemplate."*

Does everyone have an authentic golf swing?

No, but everyone has an authentic motion.

While much has been written about every golfer having their own *natural* or *authentic* golf swing, it has never been clear on exactly how you determine what that swing is. After years of working on your golf swing, how can you determine which parts of your swing are natural and which parts are contrived?

In the dictionary, *natural* is defined as, "Not acquired; inherent". No one is born with the *inherent* ability to hit and control the flight of a golf ball. You learn how to hit a golf ball through a natural process of trial and error; just as you learn all other physical skills. You eventually find a method that works for you and over time that method will *feel natural* to you. So does that method reflect your natural swing? No. There is nothing natural about methods or techniques.

There is, however, something very *natural* about the way some players swing a golf club. Regardless of the method they employ, you can sense something *authentic* about their motion; an *effortlessness* that's related to something *deeper* than technique. That something is *tempo* and *balance*, two inherent traits.

It's *natural* for us to stay in balance, and it's *natural* for us to walk, talk, and move at a certain tempo. In the dictionary, *authentic* is defined as, "of undisputed origin; genuine". When you watch a player swing in perfect balance and at their natural tempo, you can sense the *authenticity* of their motion.

You can also sense *forced effort* when watching a poor player's unbalanced thrashing movement. It's not natural to throw yourself off-balance or to swing off-tempo. That's because *conscious manipulation* is not the natural process for accomplishing a physical task.

Regardless of the technique or method you employ, you should always strive to make an *authentic* motion; to swing at your natural tempo, in balance, and free of forced effort. This is why some instructors will tell their students to *allow their natural tempo to guide their swing motion.* They're trying to teach their students how to accomplish the physical task of hitting a golf ball in a more natural manner.

How do I learn to swing in balance and at my natural tempo?

Replace thinking and trying with intention and allowing.

When you move in balance and at your natural tempo, you don't *feel* anything; which is why you'll often hear players say they don't feel anything when they're swinging their best.

Balance and tempo are natural traits. So why would you have to be taught how to swing a golf club in a manner that should be natural?

Through over thinking and trying to control your swing motion, you'll move yourself off-balance and out of rhythm. With a small adjustment here and there, over time you can find yourself tied up into a knot. Add the tension that comes from over thinking and suddenly swinging a golf club can become a very difficult task. While you don't feel yourself moving in balance and at your natural tempo, you can certainly feel the *discomfort* of swinging a golf club off-balance or out of rhythm.

The legendary swing instructor Ernest Jones was a strong advocate of swinging the golf club in the most natural manner possible. Balance and tempo were the cornerstones of his teaching philosophy. He once wrote, *"Perfection is achieved not when there is no longer anything to add, but when there is no longer anything to take away."* The things he believed should be *taken away* from the golf swing are all related to *over thinking* and *trying*.

That's how you should approach *regaining* your natural tempo and balance. **When you take away *thinking* and *trying*, you're left with the natural approach of simply creating an *intention* and *allowing* the body to respond to that intention.**

On balance, Jones writes, *"Only when we insist on considering that balance comes about by a transfer of weight, by a conscious effort – or worst yet, series of efforts – does it become a perplexing and annoying problem."*

When you walk, you do so in balance and at your natural tempo. Do you *try* to walk in balance and *think* about you natural tempo? No. You just form the *intention* of moving from point A to point B and *allow* your body to do it.

A good golf coach will guide their students into making a more natural swing motion through:

Emphasizing the importance of a more balanced address position

Teaching them how to swing without thought and in doing so maintain their natural low center of gravity

Teaching them the value of uniform grip pressure and swinging without tension

Teaching them how to initiate their swing motion in balance at their natural tempo

Teaching them how to allow their swing to unfold without effort

Teaching them how a balanced finish reflects a balanced and properly paced swing.

Does the flight of the ball tell me how I swung?

No.

You can swing a golf club many different ways and create the same ball flight. Therefore, ball flight cannot tell you how you swung. *Ball flight does, however, tell you how the clubface made contact with the golf ball and that's all you need to know.*

I refer to how the clubface makes contact with the ball as *impact dynamics*; and I always view ball flight from the perspective of how contact was made. Most golfers don't. Most golfers prefer to relate ball flight entirely to *swing motion.* For them, a poor shot will always be the result of a swing flaw. A slice will be the result of *swinging over the top*, or *swinging too fast*, or *gripping too tight*, or *moving their head on the downswing*, or one of a hundred other things. The problem is that their diagnosis is almost always wrong.

Actually, there is only one way to create slice spin – at impact, the clubface is *open* (heel leading toe) to the path the clubhead is traveling. With that understanding, the flaw becomes much easier to deal with.

You can't see your swing, you can only *feel* it. Unfortunately, what you *feel* is happening is often not happening at all. In truth, after you've swung, all you can do is make an educated *guess* at how you swung. Any adjustments would therefore be based on a guess. That's what normally happens and that's a major reason golfers fail to improve.

On the other hand, through observing the flight of the ball, the divot, and the impact location on the clubface, a knowledgeable golfer will understand *exactly* how contact was made. There's no guesswork involved and adjustments are always based on fact.

What do I need to understand about ball flight?

The impact dynamics that create it.

Understanding the physics of exactly how impact dynamics create ball flight can be quite confusing. That's because there are so many *interrelated* factors to consider. As in every other aspect of golf, overanalyzing the science is a waste of time. You should, however, be able to answer the following four questions:

What are ideal Impact Dynamics?

Ideally, at impact, the clubhead will be traveling straight down the target-line, the clubface would be perpendicular to the target line, and contact would be made in the center of the clubface. When contact is *square and centered*, a maximum amount of energy would be transferred to the ball and the ball would launch off the clubface and travel straight toward the target without sidespin.

That's the ball flight all golfers should strive for. That's the goal.

How does the path of the clubhead influence the initial direction of the ball?

When contact is made on the clubface, the ball will take off in the *general direction* the clubhead is traveling. If the clubhead is traveling straight down the target line, the ball will take off in the *general direction* of the target. If the clubhead is traveling on a line to either the left or right of the target, the ball will take off in the *general direction* of that line. I say *general direction* because the alignment of the clubface will also influence the initial direction of flight.

How does the alignment of the clubface influence the flight of the ball?

With regards to impact dynamics, the alignment of the clubface is the most important consideration. It has a direct influence over the entire flight of the ball.

If, at impact, the clubface is square (perpendicular) to the path the clubhead, no sidespin will be imparted onto the ball and the ball will launch off the clubface straight and *directly in-line with the path of the clubhead*.

If, at impact, the clubface is not square to the path of the clubhead, *sidespin* will be imparted onto the ball. *The ball will spin in the direction the clubface is aligned.* The more the clubface is misaligned, the faster the ball will spin and the farther *sideways* it will travel.

The alignment of the clubface will also influence the initial direction of the ball flight. If a right-handed golfer makes contact with the clubface *open* (heel leading toe) to the path of the clubhead, the ball will launch off the clubface slightly to the right of the direction the clubhead is moving. The degree is determined by how far to the right the clubface is aligned.

The ball is moving fastest just after impact. As the ball slows, sidespin starts to influence its flight to a greater extent. The ball will take off on a line determined by both the path of the clubhead and the alignment of the clubface. Then, as it slows, it will move sideways in the direction the clubface was aligned at impact.

How does the impact location on the clubface affect both distance and accuracy?

Have you ever noticed how much the carry distance can vary with the same club? How sometimes a *seemingly* well struck iron will fall 10 yards shorter than anticipated. It's largely related to where on the clubface you're making contact.

If you don't make contact in the center of the clubface (in-line with the clubhead's center of gravity), the clubhead will twist at impact, and the ball will travel *off-line and a shorter distance* than anticipated. Most golfers believe the shaft will prevent the clubhead from twisting at impact. It won't.

While the shaft delivers the clubhead to the ball, it does not stabilize the clubhead at impact. In fact, the clubhead responds to impact as though it was not even connected to the shaft. In Alister Cochrain's book *The Search for the Perfect Swing*, it is written, *"The clubhead responds to impact as though it were traveling through space alone, independent of the shaft"*. This is because the ball is only in contact with the clubface for approximately 9/10,000[th] of a second. By the time the shaft stabilizes the clubhead the ball has already gone.

The speed of the clubhead and the impact location on the clubface will determine how much energy is transferred to the ball. You'll carry the ball farther with added clubhead speed *only* if you're able to maintain square and centered contact.

For example, with a driver, one mile-per-hour of clubhead speed equates to slightly less than two yards of carry distance. In other words, a golfer who swings his driver head at 90 miles-per-hour will carry his drives almost 10 yards farther than a golfer with 85 miles-per-hour head speed. *But, that's only if he's able to make square and centered contact.* If he misses the sweetspot by an inch, the clubhead will turn at impact and he'll lose about 15% of his carry distance.

This is why golfers with slower swing speeds are sometimes able to hit the ball farther than golfers with faster swing speeds. Their quality of contact is better.

You'll find that your ball-striking will become more consistent if you make it a habit to view ball flight primarily from the perspective of *impact dynamics,* instead of *swing motion.* That's because your adjustments will always be based on fact, not guesswork.

Why is it that no matter how many lessons I take, I always need more?

You're never taught how to manage your swing.

Let's break down swing instruction into two areas, *Setup position* and *Swing Motion*.

> *Setup Position* – The student is taught how to grip the club and how to align and position the various parts of the body prior to swinging.

> *Swing Motion* – The student is taught how *balanced movements* of the body, arms, and wrists create a golf swing.

Quite often, by the end of the lesson, the student will be striking the ball better. That's because a good golf instructor will have the student making a more balanced swing motion *around* a better setup position.

Unfortunately, the swing tips the student learned during the lesson may not be effective the next time the student plays golf. That's because the next time the student plays golf his swing might be out of balance for a different reason. So back to the instructor the student goes. And, because his swing keeps changing, this cycle will go on until the student eventually gets frustrated and gives up on improving.

The problem in this scenario is not with the quality of the instruction, but that the instruction is incomplete. Most instructors only teach

Setup Position and *Swing Motion*. After that, the teaching stops and the focus shifts to the process of *keeping* the student's swing in balance through periodic adjustments; which translates into a never-ending series of lessons.

What's not taught, and what the student really needs to learn, is how to *manage their golf swing*. With that knowledge, the student can keep her swing in balance without the help of an instructor. She can become her own coach.

Yes, it's true that you can't see yourself swing, but you don't have to. Every time you hit a golf ball you get immediate feedback. The impact location on the clubface, the divot and the ball flight will supply you with all the information you need.

> **Managing the Golf Swing** – The student is taught how to form an intention, setup to the ball, align herself and swing at her natural tempo. Then, through observing the divot, the ball flight and the impact location on the clubface, the student is taught how to (if needed) make *slight adjustments* to her setup position to bring it into balance with the swing motion she's creating on that particular day.

Golfers can be taught to understand and manage their own swing, because their swing motion will tend to move out of balance in a relatively consistent manner. Jack Nicklaus writes, *"I'm much better off by myself. When Jack Grout taught me to play, he taught me to correct myself. Frankly, I've probably had too many teachers."*

Why does "One Swing for Everything" not work for me?

Because a golfer cannot apply the same swing thoughts to every type of swing.

One swing golf has been a popular teaching philosophy for decades. The idea is that you only have to learn one golf swing and that you can use that one swing to hit any club. Theoretically, you should be able to hit a 3-iron just as easily as you hit a 9-iron, because it's the same swing. Teachers who embrace this philosophy love to say things like, *"Why make golf more complicated than it already is? Just because you have 13 clubs doesn't mean you have to learn 13 swings. You only need to learn one swing. With that one swing you can hit every club in the bag!"*

It is certainly true that on all full golf swings the body turns back and forth, the arms swing up and down, and the wrists cock upward and release. That, however, is about all you can say. From that, it's quite a leap to conclude that one swing is all you'll ever need.

The *one swing for everything* approach sounds great; the problem is that it doesn't work. Instead of simplifying the game, it makes the game more confusing and frustrating.

Like it or not, most of us play golf through using swing thoughts. When addressing the ball, or during the swing motion, we're thinking about something that we feel will help us make the shot. It might be a tip we just read about or a thought that worked well in the past. If *one swing golf* actually worked, we'd be able to use the same swing thoughts for every shot. That's when the problems start.

I grew up watching Johnny Miller and Jack Nicklaus play golf. They were my favorite players on tour and when I played golf I tried to emulate their swings. When I thought about Miller's quick wrist break and upright swing, I had a lot of success with my wedges and short irons but no success with my driver or fairway woods. When my swing thoughts centered on Nicklaus's delayed wrist break and full extension on the takeaway, I hit my driver and fairway metals great but my wedges and short irons poorly.

Generally speaking, many of the swing thoughts that work well for long sweeping swings (drivers and fairway metals) will not work at all for short descending swings (short irons and wedges). Furthermore, the traditional set make-up is based on a changing swing, not *one swing for everything*. The driver, fairway metals and hybrid clubs are designed to be played with a *sweeping swing*, the wedges and short irons are designed to be played with a *descending swing*, and the middle and long irons are designed to be played with somewhat of a *neutral swing* (slightly descending).

Advocates of *One Swing Golf* will argue that the golfer can alter her angle of approach through simply altering her stance and ball position. With a wedge she'll play the ball approximately in the middle or back of a relatively narrow and open stance. Then, as the clubs get longer, she'll progressively widen and square her stance, while moving the ball progressively forward to promote a more sweeping angle of approach.

In other words, she'll still use one swing, just thirteen different address positions. Each position will supposedly insure the proper angle of approach.

That sounds nice but it just doesn't work. Besides the obvious fact that no golfer is going to learn 13 different address positions, changing the stance and ball position isn't enough. Regardless of how she addresses the ball, her mental approach to hitting a wedge has to be different than the approach she uses to hit a driver. Her swing thoughts will have to be different because the swing motion is different.

One swing for everything **is an overly simplified approach to playing golf that teachers like because it sounds logical, it's easy to sell and it's easy to teach. Unfortunately it doesn't work.**

How many times do I have to change my swing before I get better?

Continually learning different ways to hit a golf ball has little to do with becoming a better golfer.

Books, magazines and videos provide us with a never-ending supply of swing tips. Every time we try to incorporate one of these tips into our swing, what are we *really* doing? We're just learning a different way to hit a golf ball.

That's fine but, in the long run, what are we accomplishing? We all know that there's an endless number of ways to hit a golf ball. How many times have you, in some way, tried to change your swing? Ten times? One hundred times? In my early years, I think I tried to change my swing about a thousand times!

Unfortunately, most golfers equate swing changes with improvement. Through continually implementing swing tips they, at some level, believe themselves to be in a continual state of improvement. Actually, they're in a continual state of running in circles.

You can lower your average score with your current golf swing, ability and equipment. All you have to do is learn how to play the game better. You probably haven't heard much about *learning to play the game better* because it's not a popular topic with golf club manufacturers or swing gurus. In the final set of questions I'll give you a glimpse of what, I believe, it's all about.

A few points to remember about your golf swing

Annika Sorenstam once said, *"So many people try to make golf harder than it is."* That statement rings especially true with regards to swinging a golf club. The next time you find yourself struggling with your golf swing, remember a few of the following points:

- **There is no limit to the number of ways to effectively swing a golf club. It's *natural* for everyone to swing differently and it's a *waste of time* trying to swing like someone else.**

- **Despite what you might hear from the golf industry, there is no *one best way* to do anything. There is only the way that works *best for you*.**

- **You're never going to swing exactly the same way twice and you don't have to, *so stop trying*. Golf is not about static conditions and perfect mechanical repetition. It's about changing circumstances and your ability to adapt to those circumstances.**

- **If your alignment or setup position changes, your swing motion will change. *It has to change*. While golfers wonder why their swing motion keeps changing, they should be wondering why their alignment and setup position keep changing.**

- **Poor shots stimulate subconscious corrections. You need to fully accept that if you don't consciously control both your setup position and alignment, *they'll keep changing*.**

- You're not a *mechanical* swing machine, you're a *human* swing machine. Therefore, even if you setup to the ball and align yourself perfectly, you'll still swing bad if you think bad.

- You can't *directly* control your swing motion because it moves faster than you can think. You can only control it *indirectly*. That's done through focusing *exclusively* on the four things you can control – *how you setup to the ball, your intention, how you initiate your swing, and the tempo of your swing.*

- The golf swing is a continuous motion that you should initiate and allow to unfold as naturally as possible. That means in-balance, at your natural tempo, and free of conscious manipulation.

- The best way to swing a golf club will always be without thought. Without thought, tension and effort disappear and your swing returns to being a natural *effortless* response to your intention.

- You only need a general understanding of swing mechanics. You need to know just enough to keep your rational mind *satisfied and quiet.*

- No one is born with a natural golf swing, but everyone has an authentic motion. That motion would be at their natural tempo, in balance, and without forced effort.

- You can learn to swing in balance and at your natural tempo when you learn to replace *thinking* and *trying* with *intention* and *allowing.*

- You can swing a golf club many different ways and create the same ball flight. Therefore, ball flight *cannot* tell you how you swung. Ball flight does, however, reveal how the clubface made contact with the golf ball – *which is all you need to know.*

- **All golfers should understand how *impact dynamics* create ball flight.**

- **If you never learn how to *manage* your swing, you'll always need more lessons.**

- **Using *one swing for everything* doesn't work because you can't apply the same mental approach to every type of swing.**

- **Continually learning different ways to hit a golf ball has nothing to do with becoming a better golfer. If you want to lower your average score, you'll have to learn how to *play the game better.***

So if you've been running in circles, in search for a better golf swing, it's time to get off the merry-go-round. Take a deep breath and remember my favorite quote from the king, Arnold Palmer, *"The swing is the easiest part of golf. Once you've got the right grip and if you hold your head steady, it is almost impossible to swing badly."*

PART THREE

QUESTIONS
you should be asking about
PLAYING BETTER GOLF

People know what they do; they frequently know why they do what they do; but what they don't know is what what they do does.

- Michel Foucault
French Philosopher

Golf is at least fifty percent mental game, and if you recognize that it is the mind that prompts us physically, then we can almost say that golf is entirely a mental game

- Peter Thomson
5 time British Open Champion

How well do I know how to play golf?

Not nearly as well as you think you do.

When I tell golfers they need to learn to play the game better they argue with me, especially the low handicappers and local professionals. They roll their eyes and explain that they already know how to play golf and that their problem lies with either their *swing* or their *equipment.*

As I write this book, the number one player in the world is Tiger Woods. He plays with, what he considers to be, the absolute best equipment available. Now tell me, if you had Tiger Woods' physical ability and equipment, would you be the number one player in the world?

No. In fact you wouldn't get through the first round of the PGA Tour qualifying school. *That's because having talent is one thing and directing that talent is another.* Which is something few golfers seem to understand.

While golfers love to buy new golf clubs and analyze their swing motion, they give little thought to the far more important subjects of shot selection, intention, setup position, alignment, and focus.

The best golfers have much in common with the best pool players. The best pool players may not have the strongest break, the most expensive cue, or even the smoothest stroke. They do, however, fully understand the importance of optimal shot selection, intention and focus. They understand that pool (like golf) is a game of position. The goal of every shot, is to *leave* an ideal position from which to play the next shot.

The best pool players also understand that, regardless of how many shots they're able to foresee in advance, the most important shot is always the one they're playing. You can actually sense their focus riveted on the single intention of perfectly executing the shot at hand. They're great players because they have a deep understanding of *how the game should be played.*

When it comes to understanding how golf should be played, you've probably only scratched the surface. **Even with your current equipment and ability, your average score would be lower (possibly significantly lower) if you just knew how to play the game better.**

How do I lower my average score?

Replace a few penalizing shots with average shots.

You don't score lower by hitting more *great shots*. You do it by hitting fewer *penalizing shots*. That's because penalizing shots hurt your score more than great shots help your score.

I refer to penalizing shots as those that add *additional* stokes to your score. For example, let us say you're playing a 380-yard straight-a-way Par-4. The fairway is bordered by thick trees on the right and out-of-bounds on the left. The green is guarded in front by a very deep bunker and to the right by a small pond.

If you hook your tee-shot out of bounds, you're going to have to replay your shot plus take a one shot penalty. If you slice your tee-shot into the thick trees you're probably going to waste a shot pitching the ball back onto the fairway. Either a bad hook or a bad slice will cost you *additional* strokes.

So what happens if you hit a great 250-yard drive straight down the middle of the fairway, 20 yards farther than your normal drive? Do you get to take a stroke off your score? No, you're just 20 yards closer to the green than you normally are, making your second shot slightly easier.

If you slice your second shot into the pond, it's going to cost you a one-stroke penalty to drop out. If you hit your second shot into the deep bunker in front of the green it will probably cost you at least one additional shot to just get the ball out. Again, bad shots cost you *additional* strokes.

So what happens if you hit a great second shot about 15 feet from the pin? Well, you're certainly closer to the pin than you normally are, but your chances of making the putt are quite small. The average golfer makes a 15 foot putt less than one time out of ten.

On this particular hole, you could make your average 230-yard tee-shot, your average 150-yard second shot next to the green, an average chip and putt and make a score of 4. You can also make a great 250-yard drive, an excellent 130-yard second shot and a great putt that just lips out and you still make a score of 4. Any penalizing shots along the way will quickly increase your score. *The idea in golf is to add stokes slowly, not quickly.*

I've seen many players break par without hitting one truly exceptional shot. It's very possible that you could make the lowest score in your life without hitting a single exceptional shot.

In his classic book *How to Play Your Best Golf All The Time,* the legendary Tommy Armour states, *"It is not solely the capacity to make great shots that make champions, but the essential quality of making very few bad shots."*

In *Harvey Penick's Little Red Book,* Penick writes, *"The important question is not how good your good shots are – it's how bad are your bad ones?"*

You don't need to hit more great shots to lower your average score. You just need to replace a few penalizing shots with average shots. **And you can start doing it immediately.**

How do I replace penalizing shots with average shots?

Learn to play every shot with a higher degree of purpose.

Researchers tell us that we have about sixty thousand thoughts a day, and that we keep thinking the same sixty thousand thoughts. Which is why our lives tend to evolve into such a rut.

I don't know how many thoughts the average golfer has during a round of golf, but I guarantee you, they don't change much. Golfers generally approach each shot with some version of the same three thoughts – *Select a club, Aim at the flag, Fire.* That approach allows them to play golf with the least amount of effort possible. They could play in their sleep and, in a sense, that's exactly what they do. Very little attention is given to shot selection, intention, setup position, alignment, or focus. **I refer to this style of play as *aimless* and when you play *aimless golf* you hit a lot of penalizing shots.**

The opposite of aimless golf is playing golf *with purpose*, a style of play in which a great deal of attention is given to the *approach to every shot*. **And when you play golf *with purpose* you hit fewer penalizing shots. It's that simple.**

Playing golf *with purpose* is often referred to as playing golf *one shot at a time.* And even the most experienced professionals often have to remind themselves to do it. Bobby Jones wrote, *"It is nothing new or original to say that golf is played one stroke at a time. But it took me years to realize it."*

Contrary to what most golfers believe, playing golf *one shot at a time* does not require a lot of effort. In fact, once you organize your thinking, it requires less than 30 seconds of thought per shot. The key is to develop an approach that is both *complete* (to avoid penalizing shots) and *simple* (so you'll apply it to every shot).

Your approach to a shot is *complete* when each of the *controllable* aspects of shotmaking is given appropriate consideration. Again, that would include *shot selection, intention, setup position, alignment, and focus.*

That sounds like a lot to consider on every shot, and it is. That's why the best players develop a *shotmaking routine* that makes the process almost automatic. They employ the same series of steps for every shot. Something similar to this:

Shot Selection and Intention

Before addressing the ball, they determine the *exact shot* they're attempting to create, form a clear and positive intention to create it, and use some technique to strengthen that intention.

Setup Position and Alignment

While focused on their target, they employ an *established personal routine* for getting themselves correctly aligned and properly set up to the ball.

Focus

Shifting their focus to the ball, they form the intention of making square and centered contact, clear their mind, and allow their body to *spontaneously and naturally* respond to that intention.

Barring unusual circumstances, the entire shotmaking routine should take less than 30 seconds. And you can normally start the process while waiting for your playing partners to hit their shots.

The trick is to give each shot the required amount of attention. Giving a single shot 30 seconds of organized thought is not difficult. Playing every shot in the round *with that degree of purpose* requires more effort than most golfers are willing to give.

But how much effort does it really take to *think* for a few seconds? Even when you play aimless golf, you're always going to *determine* the type of shot you're going to play, create some sort of *intention, setup to the ball* in some manner, and *think* about something while you're swinging. The question is do you want to approach the endeavors *aimlessly* or *with purpose*? Do you want to hit more penalizing shots or fewer?

You can reduce the number of penalizing shots you hit per round immediately. All you have to do is play *every shot* with a higher degree of purpose.

What is the essence of good golf?

Distance Control.

While the average golfer remains fixated on trying to hit the ball farther, the essence of good golf is *distance control* – not raw distance. The long hitter's actual advantage will always be relative to his ability to *control* his distances.

The importance of distance control can be clearly illustrated in every aspect of the game. For example, experienced golfers seldom misread the line of a putt by as much as a foot. And when they miss-hit a putt, they'll generally only miss their intended line by a few inches. They do, however, regularly misjudge the distance of a putt by several feet.

The lack of distance control becomes more evident with chips and simple pitch shots. While the average golfer hits these shots relatively straight, he'll routinely leave them 10 to 20 feet short or long of the cup. Wouldn't it be better to misread the line by 3 or 4 feet and hit the shot the correct distance?

On full shots most golfers lose distance control because they attempt to hit every club as far as possible. What value is it to swing your 7-iron hard and, depending on how you make contact, hit it somewhere between 130 and 150 yards? Wouldn't it obviously be better to know that with a controlled swing you carry your 7-iron approximately 140 yards, your 6-iron 150 yards, and your 8-iron 130 yards?

With distance control, you can learn better course management and gain the ability to immediately lower your scores. Without distance control, you have little hope for real improvement.

How do I achieve distance control?

Through playing with golf clubs that promote distance control and through focusing more on quality contact than swing mechanics and clubhead speed.

You need to play with the clubs with which you're able to make square and centered contact and achieve a playable trajectory the highest percentage of time. This may require not only altering your club specifications but, more importantly, your *set composition.* One of the primary keys to distance control is to play with the clubs that are *easy for you to use.* That may not sound *high-tech,* but it's the truth. Properly fit golf clubs can be acquired through working with a *qualified* clubfitter.

Then, during your warm-up and practice sessions, instead of focusing on your swing mechanics (body) and your clubhead speed (distance), you need to focus on improving the *quality and consistency* of your ball-striking (impact dynamics). That can be accomplished through repeatedly asking yourself the following questions:

Where am I making contact on the clubface today?

You maximize the transfer of energy to the golf ball when you make contact in the center of the clubface (in-line with the clubhead's center of gravity). The easiest way to become aware of where you're making contact is to practice with impact tape. When playing, you can usually tell by feel or looking at the clubface.

When you make contact toward the toe or heel of the clubface, the clubhead will turn at impact and you'll feel the vibration in your hands. There is a distinctive feel associated with where you make contact on the clubface. With a little effort, you can train yourself to feel where you're making contact on every shot. *If you find, on a given day, that you're repeatedly making contact toward either the heel or toe, you can bring it to center through adjusting your setup position.*

Where is the bottom of my swing arc today?

Your divots not only reveal the direction the clubhead was traveling at impact, but also the bottom of the swing arc. You need to understand where your swing is bottoming out, so you can position the ball accordingly at address.

Ball position is probably the most underrated aspect of your setup position. When hitting an iron, you want to position the ball very slightly behind the bottom of your swing arc; slightly behind where you normally take a divot. Doing so will insure that you strike the ball with a downward blow that'll create added backswing. The added backspin will provide added trajectory and insure that the ball lands softly.

Clubs that are designed with a lower center of gravity (fairway metals and hybrids) are meant to be played with a sweeping motion. Contact is made with the club moving either parallel to the ground or very slightly downward. For these clubs, the ball should be positioned at the bottom of the swing arc.

The driver is teed-up and positioned forward in the stance so contact can be made with the clubhead ascending upward.

Regardless of the club you're using, for quality contact, proper ball position is critical. That's why you have to know where your swing is bottoming out on a given day. Like every other aspect of your swing motion, the bottom of your swing arc is subject to change slightly on a daily basis.

On what line is the clubhead moving today?

Your divot or the initial direction of the ball will tell you the line on which the clubhead was moving at impact. You should strive to have the clubhead moving straight down the target line. If it's not, you'll probably have to make an adjustment to your setup position. The alignment of your shoulders and ball position will greatly influence the path of the clubhead.

Where am I squaring the clubface today?

To insure that your ball is spinning toward your target, you should strive to have the clubface square or perpendicular to the target line at impact.

If the ball is spinning away from the target it's because the clubface was either too open (heel leading toe) or too closed (toe leading heel) at impact. You can alter the alignment of the clubface at impact through making a slight adjustment to your grip, ball position, or how you initiate your swing motion.

What caused that ball flight?

You should always define ball flight in terms of impact dynamics not swing motion. Remember, you can never know exactly how you swung because you can't see yourself swing. The flight of the ball will, however, perfectly reflect impact dynamics.

If a right-handed golfer hits a pull hook (ball starts on a line left of the target and then hooks further left of the target) he knows exactly how the clubhead was moving and how the clubface was aligned at impact. The clubhead was moving on a line left of the target and the clubface was closed (toe leading heel) to the direction the clubhead was moving.

Because there is no guesswork involved, he can deal with the problem in a more direct manner.

How do I carry the ball that many yards without effort?

When practicing, instead of trying to maximize the carry distance of every club, try to identify the approximate carry distance of every club when you swing at your natural tempo. Your average shot is always going to be a slight miss-hit, so make your estimates conservative.

Then put your conclusions in writing and practice hitting those numbers – not increasing those numbers. The goal is to learn how to carry the ball a specific distance at a playable trajectory with the least amount of effort. **The number on the club you use does not matter.**

Through staying centered on these questions, you'll start to perceive the game differently. Your fixation on *raw distance* will slowly diminish, as you give more consideration to the *quality and consistency* of your ball-striking. Instead of focusing exclusively on *swing mechanics,* your attention will shift to *impact dynamics*. You'll acquire *added distance control* and you'll find yourself on the road to becoming a better golfer.

What should be my primary objective on every swing?

Square and Centered Contact.

The essence of good golf is distance control, and the key to distance control is a consistent quality of contact. **Since ideal contact is *square and centered*, your primary goal on every swing should be square and centered contact.** Contact made in the *center* of a clubface that's *square* to the target. Whether you're stroking a putt, hitting a chip, or making a full swing, your primary goal should always be the same – square and centered contact.

The successful execution of every shot will be dependent on the *quality of contact*. **Most golfers, however, believe that the successful execution of every shot will always be dependent on the *quality of swing*.** They believe that a quality swing *automatically* produces quality contact, so they remain focused on their swing.

When your primary objective is to make a *quality golf swing*, you're attempting to do something you can't *exactly* define. Furthermore, you're hoping that quality contact somehow *just happens* as a result of *trying* doing something you can't quite define. That's a hopelessly backwards perspective that never works for very long.

On the other hand, when your primary objective is *square and centered contact,* you're attempting to do something that is easily definable. Plus, you don't have to worry about *how you do it*, because it doesn't matter *how you do it*.

Peter Croker explains in his book, *Golf the Natural Way*, that golf is a *two-target game*. The *clubhead's target* is the ball and the *ball's target* is the hole (or a position on the fairway or green). If the clubhead achieves its goal (square and centered contact) the ball will achieve its goal (fly to the target).

Make square and centered contact your primary goal on every shot. Then clear your mind, stay present and let your body do it.

Why does always aiming directly at the flag add strokes to my score?

You'll hit into penalizing situations more often.

Have you ever noticed how the best players seem to save par almost every time they miss a green? Well, it's not just because their short games are good. It's because they (unlike most golfers) leave themselves in positions from where it's *easy* to get up and down. On their approach shots to the green they play away from the most severe penalizing situations. **When you optimize your shot selection, you don't have to hit great shots to score well.**

For example, imagine you're playing your second shot on a Par-4 to a wide and deep green. The flag's tucked in the front right hand corner of the green behind a large sand trap. You've got a great lie in the middle of the fairway and you're exactly 145 yards from the hole. You *know* you hit a full 7-iron exactly 145 yards, so how do you play the shot?

Most golfers will think of this situation as a birdie opportunity because the lie is perfect and the distance appears to be ideal. They'll take out their 7-iron, aim dead at the pin and probably end up in a penalizing situation. Why?

The first problem is that golfers tend to overestimate the distance they hit each club. When they say they hit their 7-iron exactly 145 yards, what they really mean is that *when they make perfect contact* their 7-iron will travel 145 yards. What golfers fail to realize is that making perfect contact is not at all the norm. All golfers are going to miss-hit their shot, to some degree, the great majority of the time. If they miss the center of the clubface by half an inch (toward either the toe or heel), the 145-yard 7-iron will carry less than 140 yards. If they miss the center of the clubface by an inch (which they often do), the 7-iron will carry closer to 130 yards. Have you ever noticed that hazards in the front of the green catch a lot more balls than hazards in the back of the green? It's not just a coincidence.

The second problem is that golfers believe they hit the ball a lot straighter than they actually do. They don't hit many greens in regulation because they don't hit the ball very straight. In fact, from 145 yards out, average golfers could easily miss their target 25 yards to the left or right. However, they remember the perfectly straight 7-iron they once hit, so that becomes their standard for 7-iron accuracy – perfectly straight.

If, in this example, you aim at the flag and happen to miss your 7-iron slightly to the right (and you're lucky enough to carry the bunker) you'll end up with a very difficult chip because you'll have no green to work with. You'll have to chip the ball onto the green and have it stop quickly, which can be difficult to do. **Putting yourself in this position is called *short-siding*, and better golfers make every effort to avoid it.** It would have been much better to miss the green to the left. You would have been farther from the hole, but you would have a lot of green to work with. The chip would have been much easier. With a 7-iron aimed directly at the flag, your only hope is to hit it perfect (good luck) or hit it left and hard enough to carry the bunker.

What happens if you do hit the 7-iron perfect? If you happen to hit a great 7-iron, 10 to 15 feet from the flag, congratulations - you just hit a great shot! Unfortunately, you're still going to miss the putt the vast majority of the time. Not much of a reward for such a gamble.

That's the reason why the optimal shot would have been a 6-iron aimed at the center of the green. Even if you slightly miss the 6-iron (which is going to happen almost every time), you'll still probably carry the bunker. Also, by aiming to the middle of the green, you'll give yourself a wide margin of error in both directions (which you definitely need).

While you still might end up *accidentally* hitting it close to the pin, you have greatly decreased the possibility of hitting into a penalizing situation.

Jim McLean, in his book, *Golf School*, writes, *"Jack Nicklaus played his entire career by hitting mostly to the center of the green…Amateurs go flag hunting a lot too often, and it severely hurts their scoring ability and enjoyment."*

With poor shot selection you'll continually need to hit exceptional shots. First, you'll need to hit great shots to avoid hitting into penalizing situations. Then you'll need to hit great shots to get out of penalizing situations you'll find yourself continually in.

Avoiding penalizing situations should always be your primary goal. For the most part, this is going to require forgetting about the flagstick and aiming at the middle of green. It's also going to require that you have a *realistic* understanding of the distance you carry each club and your normal degree of accuracy.

You can lower your average score simply through improving your shot selection. Whenever you select a shot that's going to require perfect execution to avoid a penalizing result, you've selected the wrong shot. **Your normal shot is going to be a slight miss-hit. You have to accept that and prepare for it.**

The legendary football coach Walter Camp once said, "In golf, as in life, the attempt to do something in one stroke that needs two is apt to result in taking three". Remember that.

What is the most important shot on every hole?

The shot you're playing.

I once read that Ben Hogan said that the most important shot on every hole was the first shot. At first thought, that seemed logical because the tee shot would determine how the balance of the hole would have to be played out.

Then I recalled a hole I had played the previous day. My friend had hit his best drive of the day on a long and difficult par-4. From the ideal location in the fairway, he was left with only a short iron to the green. After such a perfect drive, he was intent on making a birdie and he took dead aim at the flag. Unfortunately, his overly aggressive second shot came up short and into the front sand trap. Frustrated, he hit a poor sand shot and ended up making a five.

After being pleased with myself for playing my second shot conservatively to the middle of the green, I ran my approach putt several feet past the hole and also made five.

I would have to side with those that believe that the most important shot will always be the one you're playing. **Not just the tee-shot, but every shot will determine how the balance of the hole will have to be played out.**

Before I start to address the ball, what should I have already done?

Determined the specific shot you intended to create, and formed a clear and positive intention to create it.

It's unfortunate that most golfers fail to appreciate and, as a result, misuse the enormous power of intention.

Whenever you hit a particularly bad shot, ask yourself, *"What exactly was I intending to do, anyway?"* Your intention was probably something along the lines of *"Hit it hard"*, *"Keep my head down"* or *"Don't slice it"*. While all of those intentions are clear, they have nothing to do with a *specific target.*

The great Canadian golfer George Knudsen said that golf was a game of A to B. He meant that golf consisted of a series of shots, played *one at a time* and always with the *intention* of hitting to a *specific target.* Hitting from point A to point B.

Golfers, for some reason, think the best way to hit their target is by thinking about something else. Instead of thinking *A to B*, they think, *don't go to C.* It's not the same. The thought *"Don't hook it in the lake"* is not going to help you hit your drive down the center of the fairway. In fact, that thought will actually bring the lake more into play.

Sports psychologists universally agree that envisioning a positive outcome is an integral part of success; that your actions are greatly influenced by the *visions* you hold in your mind. Human beings think in

117

pictures. The thought, *"Don't hook the ball into the lake"* will create a *vision* of the ball flying into the lake. The thought, *"Don't be short"*, will create the *vision* of the putt stopping short of the hole. There's an old saying that the mind doesn't understand the word *don't*. Actually, the mind can't *envision* the word *don't*.

If you listen to a PGA touring professional talking to his caddy, you'll often hear the phrase, *"What's the number"*? The professional is asking the caddy for the exact carry yardage needed for a particular shot. The professional may not be able to guarantee that his cut 5-iron will travel exactly 187 yards, but he can establish the intent for it to travel exactly 187 yards and he knows that establishing an *exact, clear and positive intent* will enormously improve his chance of pulling off the shot. He would certainly never think, *"Don't hit it 197 yards over the green and into the back sand trap"*

To use the power of intention effectively, you need to forget about what you *don't* want to happen and focus exclusively on what you *do* want to happen. Then, after forming an *exact, clear and positive intention*, you need to develop some technique to strengthen it.

Jack Nicklaus sharpens his intention through visualizing *every shot* before he hits it. He calls it *Going to the Movies* and he outlined the steps he takes in his classic book, *Golf My Way.*Tiger Woods says he tries to *feel* the correct execution of every shot before attempting it.

It doesn't matter whether you *visualize* your intention, *feel it* in your practice swings, or just *verbalize it* before addressing the ball. The idea is to do whatever it takes to keep the intention *exact, clear and positive;* to do whatever works for you.

Just make it a goal to never again have to ask yourself, *"What exactly was I intending to do, anyway?"*

Am I present when I'm swinging?

Most golfers aren't.

The fact that all creation happens in the present moment is pretty obvious. The fact that our thoughts are almost never centered in the present moment is not so obvious. It's also a problem.

In his wonderful book, *The Power of Now*, Eckhart Tolle writes that despite the present moment being the only *reality*, our thoughts are continually centered in either the past or on the future. We allow our thoughts of the past to establish our self-image and our perception of present circumstance. Our thoughts of the future provide us with an insight as to where we might be headed.

While we constantly think about where we've been and where we're headed, we almost never think about where we are. For example, what are your thoughts when faced with a lob shot over a steep bunker to a tight pin? If you're like most golfers, your first thoughts will be centered in the past. By remembering similar experiences, you'll try to determine what chance you have of pulling off the shot. Your mind will be filled with thoughts like, *"I've never been good at this shot"* or *"The last time I had this shot I shanked it"* or *"I love this shot"*.

To consider the possible outcomes, your mind will also jump to the future with thoughts like, *"If I hit the shot fat, I'll end up in the bunker and probably make a double bogey"* or *"If I blade the shot 20 yards over the green everyone will laugh at me"* or *"If I knock this shot stiff everyone will be impressed"*.

Philip Moore

Unfortunately, none of these thoughts have anything to do with actually making the shot. The shot can't be made in the past or in the future, it has to be made in the present moment.

The golf ball, the golf club, your body, your swing, and the golf course all exist in the present moment. **Your mind, however, could be anywhere. Since all creation takes place in the present moment, that's where your mind should be fully engaged.**

Bringing yourself to the moment is one thing, staying in the moment throughout the swing motion is something else. As Bobby Jones once wrote, "*...there must be no mental daisy-picking while the shot is being played.*"

How do I stay present while the shot is being played?

You stay Aware and Empty.

Staying present on the golf course can be difficult for anyone. Especially for someone who is overly self conscious, fearful, or analytical. An over active mind consumes present moment awareness.

Being lost in thought dulls your senses. The birds can be singing and you won't *hear* them, and you can take a bite of a delicious sandwich and not *taste* it, and you can swing a golf club and not *feel* it. That's because you're more aware of what you're *thinking* than what you're *experiencing*.

Present moment awareness is the essence of Zen Buddhism. Many have found that adopting the Eastern practices of *mindfulness* and *emptiness* to be beneficial not only to their golf game, but to all aspects of their life.

A very simple definition of mindfulness would be, *intentionally being aware of and fully engaged in the present moment.*

A very simple definition of emptiness would be, *perceiving with an 'empty' mind; free of all presuppositions, judgment, and self consciousness.*

At first thought, ideas of *mindfulness* and *emptiness* appear to be para-doxical. How can you be fully aware of and engaged in the present mo-ment while maintaining an empty mind? Actually, it's our most creative state. You can observe it when watching the best dancers dance, the best singers sing, and the best golfers swing. They're fully immersed in the moment and their actions are spontaneous and natural. They don't allow *thinking* to interfere with *doing*.

While the shot is being played, you stay present through being *aware and fully engaged* in what you're doing without *thinking about* what you're doing. You create the *intention* of making square and centered contact, *focus* on the ball, and let your body *effortlessly* respond to your intention.

How does staying present help me swing better?

When you're not thinking, your swing is authentic.

In the book *Surfing the Himalayas,* Master Fwap, a fictional Buddhist monk, tells his student, *"Mindfulness is the practice of doing physical things perfectly - in a state of emptiness - in which we become consciously 'one' with whatever physical or mental activity we are currently engaged in."*

With regards to conscious thought during physical activity, Master Fwap states, *"Try always to remember that when you think about something, you separate yourself from it."*

Your swing will always unfold best when allowed to do so in the most natural and spontaneous manner, free from the interference of conscious thought. It's true that you *think about* your shot selection, forming an intention and where you're going to give your focus. There comes a point, however, when *thinking about* what you're going to do is replaced with *allowing your body* to do it.

Tiger Woods once said that he could vividly remember all of his thoughts leading up to a shot, but that he could never remember swinging. That's because he has no thoughts while he is swinging. He *empties his mind* and allows the swing to unfold in an authentic manner. He simply stays present. He often refers to it as staying *committed to the shot.*

Philip Moore

The greatest athletes *think less* when they're performing. Instead of *thinking about* what they're doing, they simply *stay aware* of what they're doing. As Dr. Bob Rotella writes in his book, *The Golfer's Mind,* *"The human organism performs best in athletics when the conscious mind is turned off."*

Am I supposed to focus on my target or my ball?

First your target then your ball.

Your body responds to both your intention and your focus. Therefore, your focus should always compliment your intention.

After determining the exact shot you *intend* to create, the first step is to get yourself properly set up to the ball and aligned to the target. Keeping your *focus* on the target greatly aids that process through giving you a constant reference point.

At some point before completely settling into your address position, your *intention should shift* to the goal of making square and centered contact with the golf ball. That's best accomplished through *shifting your focus* from the target to the ball and keeping it there throughout the swing motion.

Like every other aspect of golf, focus is not *strained* or *forced*, it is simply *given*.

What is the greatest hazard in golf?

Fear.

Sam Snead once said *"Of all the hazards, fear is the worst"*. Jack Nicklaus once wrote, *"fear of any kind is the number one enemy of all golfers, regardless of ball-striking and shot-making capabilities"*.

With fear, golf is no longer a game of A to B. Instead of being committed to a single target, we become preoccupied with where *not to go* and what *not to do*. The result being, as famed golf instructor Butch Harmon once said, *"...we get so afraid of hitting bad shots, we don't let ourselves hit good ones."*

Golfers generally underestimate the amazing effect that fear can have on their swing. I first became aware of it over 30 years ago, while going through a long period of struggling with short putts. As soon as I drew the putter head back a fearful thought would pop into my mind and negatively influence my stroke. What I found amazing was that my hands would respond to the thought seemingly on their own. Without any conscious effort, my stroke would change *in unison* with the negative thought. My stroke didn't actually *respond* to the thought, my stroke *reflected* the thought.

It's easy to see the same phenomena occur on full shots. How often have you seen two hooks followed by a slice? It's a common occurrence, even at the professional level. Imagine hooking your first two tee shots of the day deep into the trees, left of the fairway. Now you're on the third tee, looking at a long straight-a-way par-4 with a water hazard bordering the entire left side of the fairway. You try to forget about your first two tee shots and trust your swing. You once again pick a target in the middle of the fairway and try to make your normal swing. This time, however, the subconscious fear of hitting another hook surfaces; just before impact, your hands tighten and the ball goes straight right. You become immensely frustrated because you feel as though you have suddenly lost all control over your swing. You just made two severe hooks and a severe slice while trying, each time, to make a normal swing and hit the ball straight!

Fear can also affect a golfer's perception. The fear of missing the fairway will make wide fairways suddenly *appear* narrower. The fear of missing putts will make the hole suddenly *appear* smaller and make the greens *appear* more difficult to read.

So what causes fear? Short game guru Dave Pelz writes, *"Golfers who don't care never get the yips."* PGA touring professional Brad Faxon states, *"Kids have no fear when they putt. They miss it and it doesn't affect them. You've got to keep that attitude your whole life. That's my whole premise toward putting. If you care whether you miss, you're in trouble."*

Eckhart Tolle writes in his book, *Practicing The Power of Now,* *"...psychological fear is always of something that might happen, not of something that is happening now. You are in the here and now, while your mind is in the future....You can always cope with the present moment, but you cannot cope with something that is only a mind projection – you cannot cope with the future."*

Fear arises when your mind jumps into the future and considers the consequences of what might happen. When you place too much importance on outcome, it becomes impossible to stay in the present moment and fully committed to the shot; impossible to let go and trust your swing.

So how do you deal with fear? That question should be replaced with, *how do you forget about what might happen and keep your focus entirely in the present moment?*

I wish there was a simple answer. Volumes have been written on the subject. Like everything else in golf, it appears that you have to find your own way. I'm discussing fear primarily to illustrate just another aspect of golf that can have a far greater influence on your golf game than equipment or swing mechanics.

How do I prevent myself from improving?

Through trying to consciously manipulate your swing motion.

Ben Crenshaw, in his video, *The Art of Putting*, stated he was a fatalistic putter. In other words, after he chose his line, addressed the ball and made the best stoke possible, whatever happened, just happened. After the ball left the putter face, he had no control over it and therefore didn't worry about it. Some days they go in and some days they don't. He had done all he could do.

You need to become a fatalistic golfer. As long as you're doing all you can do, why worry about the rest? All you can do is select the proper shot, form a clear intention to create it, properly address the ball, establish the intention of making square and centered contact, and let go.

The problem is that most golfers can't *let go*. They worry about the shot and, as a result, try to manipulate the swing motion. In doing so, they destroy the natural process. As Harvey Penick once said, *"Thinking too much about how you are doing when you are doing is disastrous."*

George Knudsen writes in his book, *Natural Golf*, that the golfer has to *"Give up control to gain control"*. In other words you can't achieve control over the flight of the golf ball by trying to consciously control the swing motion. You need to let the swing unfold naturally. Knudsen explains, *"...golf is a 'passive' game, one in which we LET most things happen rather than MAKE them happen."*

The legendary Moe Norman, who many consider to be the greatest ball striker of all time, would say, *"Let the body enjoy the shot. That's the biggest word in golf, let"*. In other words, just let go and enjoy the freedom of an unrestricted swing. He defined the game of golf as "...*hitting an object to a defined target area with the least amount of effort and an alert attitude of indifference."* To Moe, golf was certainly not about effort, forcing, or worry.

Bobby Jones wrote, *"I believe most sincerely that the impulse to steer, born of anxiety, is accountable for almost every really bad shot."*

The swing motion will unfold best if you just allow it to. If you just get out of the way and let it happen. **Focused on making square and centered contact, you don't think about *how* your body is going to do it, just *allow* your body to do it.**

When attempting to drive a nail into a wall, you focus entirely on making square contact with the head of the nail. You know that if you're able to make square contact you'll drive the tip of the nail straight into the wall. So with the intent of making square contact, you focus on the head of the nail and drive it into the wall. You don't worry about *how* you're going to do it, *you just allow your body to do it.* Unfortunately, this is not the approach most golfers use when hitting a golf ball. Their conscious mind tells them that they have to be thinking about *how* they're going to make square and centered contact, but that's not true.

Have you ever considered how babies are able to learn how to run, climb and swim before they're able to talk? Without being *told* how to do it (or even having the ability to *tell themselves* how to do it) babies are able to quickly learn how to accomplish and *effortlessly repeat* an endless number of physical endeavors. That's because their natural ability is not impeded by conscious thought.

It all boils down to accepting that your body is smarter than you are. I found that idea was perfectly expressed in Steven Pressfield's wonderful book, *The Legend of Bagger Vance*. The mysterious caddie Bagger Vance tells his nervous golfing friend Rannulph Junah, *"You're in your head, Junah, I need you to come down into your hands. Listen to me. Intelligence, I have told you, does not reside in the brain but in the hands. Let them do the thinking, they're far wiser than you are."*

Are severe mis-hits just part of golf?

No more than losing your focus is just part of golf.

When you play well, what's happening? You're consistently hitting shots pretty much as you intended. That's about it. We love to remember and talk about our best holes, but our best holes don't teach us much. For example, do you remember the last time you birdied a Par-4? You probably hit your drive in the fairway, just as you intended. Then you probably hit your second shot onto the green, again as you intended. Finally, you tried to make your birdie putt and you holed it. What you did was make three shots, as intended, in succession. That's all.

What's much more interesting is when the shot you create isn't close to the shot you had in mind. For example, when you intend to hit your drive down the center of the fairway, but instead slice it 30 yards out-of-bounds. What happened? Where did that shot come from? I guarantee that your driver didn't change. Neither did the ball. So what went wrong? Why did you suddenly swing differently?

Golfers generally consider really bad shots to be just part of the game; something that can't be avoided. That's not entirely true. To say that there's nothing you can do about really bad shots, is saying there's nothing you can do about losing your focus.

You may periodically lose your focus, but you can certainly train yourself to do it less often. Likewise, you may hit really bad shots, but you can certainly reduce the number of bad shots you hit per round.

How? Again, through playing golf *one shot at a time.* Through taking the time, *on every shot,* to do the things that are within your *conscious control.* Those would include:

Optimizing your shot selection.

Establishing a clear and positive intention to create that exact shot.

Setting-up to the ball and aligning yourself in the manner that perfectly compliments that exact shot.

Shifting your focus to the goal of making square and centered contact and maintain that focus throughout the swing motion.

Allowing your body to effortlessly respond to your intention.

It's called *doing all you can do,* and it takes less than 30 seconds per shot. The goal is not to eliminate mis-hits, because that's never going to happen. As Ben Hogan said, *golf is a game of mis-hits.* The goal is to reduce your number of *severe* mis-hits (penalizing shots). **Slight mis-hits are manageable, severe mis-hits are not.** *Which is why playing golf one shot at a time is so important.*

What's the quickest way to center my focus?

Forget about what you can't control.

While attempting to create a golf shot, golfers will too often allow their focus to wander into areas they have no control over. Normally:

What other golfers are thinking or doing

What their final score might be

What might happen to the ball after it leaves the clubface

Exactly how their swing is going to unfold

When you're trying to hit a golf ball, you don't have to dwell on every thought that passes through your mind. If the thought is unrelated to the shot you're attempting to create, you simply acknowledge that it's unrelated and let it pass. Then you return your focus to what you have control over – *shot selection, intention, setup position, alignment, and focus.*

Good golf requires the ability to create single-minded focus during the few seconds it takes to execute a golf shot. That focus needs to be centered exclusively on the areas within your control.

Why is it that some aspects of my game never improve?

You've developed a limiting belief system.

Albert Einstein is credited with stating that the most important decision a person can make is whether the universe is friendly or hostile. He was referring to the incredible influence of *core belief*; specifically, how that most fundamental *core belief* would directly influence how a person perceived and dealt with every circumstance in his or her life.

I have never met a highly successful individual who truly believed life was a struggle. I've also never met a struggling individual who truly believed life was a breeze.

If you're an avid golfer, you have strong core beliefs about golf, your ability to play golf, and every aspect of your game. Left alone, these beliefs can severely limit your ability to improve. Whether facing a simple three-foot putt, a tricky sand shot, or a drive onto a narrow fairway, your level of success will be determined greatly by your belief in your ability to execute that specific shot. Beliefs create vivid expectations and, as Arnold Palmer once said, *"Your performance has a way of living up to your expectations."*

This is why some aspects of your game seem to never improve. You're unable to break through a limiting belief system. As Henry Ford famously stated, *"Think you can, think you can't; either way, you'll be right."*

So how are you supposed to change a belief in your ability when the past results don't warrant it? If you've been putting poorly for years, how are you supposed to suddenly *believe* that you're a good putter?

Luckily, most golfers tend to link performance more with technique than natural ability. Through learning a significantly different technique, a golfer can develop a completely new perspective and feel for the shot they've been struggling with. In doing so, they're sometimes able to leave all the negative beliefs associated with the old technique behind them.

This is why you'll sometimes see players on the PGA Tour significantly improve after changing their swing coach. They had developed a limiting belief system, and they were able to move past it through employing a different technique. If they succeed, most observers will mistakenly attribute their success to the new coach or the trendy new technique. Actually, their success will be related far more to their new mindset. **They linked failure to their past technique and success to the new technique.** *It was that connection that made the difference.*

What is the only way to achieve day-to-day consistency?

Learn how to make day-to-day adjustments.

When golfers work on their swing, they try to incorporate permanent swing changes. They're hoping to make their swing permanently better. Experts have estimated that it would take at least 10,000 *perfect* repetitions of a new movement before that movement would become a permanent part of a golfers swing. That means months of perfect practice. That also means that you can forget about it.

Even if you had nothing else to do with your life but work on your golf swing, would it make a difference? Don't you find it curious that the job of working on your swing mechanics seems to never end? Is there really a need for a never-ending analysis of technique? Would it really help us if we had a swing instructor follow us around the golf course with a video camera?

Teachers pride themselves in being able to detect subtle changes in a players swing motion, and then being able to advise the player on how to immediately correct the change. Being an advocate of the *you're never going to swing the same way twice theory*, I wonder how important a subtle change in your swing motion really makes.

The one message I'm hoping to convey is that every time you come to the golf course, you bring a different body and a different mindset. Your physical condition, confidence, and ability to focus are always changing.

Which means that you're going to notice subtle changes in your swing motion. **You need to understand and accept that, because there's nothing you can do about it.**

I remember, almost 30 years ago, reading a book entitled *Teed Off,* by PGA Touring professional Dave Hill. Hill was a popular and very outspoken touring pro in the 1960's and 70's. This book was supposed to reflect his candid opinions about the golfing establishment. I don't remember anything about the book (I guess it wasn't all that controversial), but I vividly remember a particular photograph of Hill hitting balls on the driving range. Under the photograph Hill wrote the line, *"Finding out which way they're moving today."* What did that mean? Dave Hill was one of the top PGA Touring professionals in the world. He always knew exactly where the ball was going - or so I thought at the time.

How many times have you heard a touring professional speak of playing great one day and for some reason *losing* his or her game the next? Even Tiger Woods, who does everything possible to maintain peak mental and physical conditioning, will speak of having his *A game* one day and his *B or C game* the next.

In his book , *How I Play Golf,* Tiger Woods states, *"My swing tendencies change a bit from day to day. That's part of golf; for no discernible reason your misses might one day be pulls to the left, the next day fades a bit too far to the right. These small shifts in ball flight aren't necessarily disastrous, provided you allow for them".*

While PGA Touring professionals may not know why change occurs, they have definitely learned how to deal with it. Instead of fighting change, they expect it and adapt to it through daily adjustments. Tiger Woods and Jack Nicklaus have both spoken extensively on having to learn how to win tournaments without their best games. Nicklaus refers to the process as *playing badly well.*

When golfers strive to be more consistent through making permanent swing changes, they tend to ignore the more important need for daily adjustments. To these golfers, I like to relate the famous quote from author Ralph L. Woods, *"There are no permanent changes because change itself is permanent."*

Day-to-day consistency cannot be obtained through making a permanent change in your swing motion. It can only be achieved through learning how to manage the subtle day-to-day changes in your swing motion that will always occur.

How do I manage the subtle day-to-day changes in my swing motion?

Through making subtle changes in your shot selection, course management, and address position.

All golfers should allow the quality of their ball-striking on a given day to influence their shot selection and course management. Some players will go a step farther and, if needed, make slight adjustments to their setup position to create a more controllable ball flight.

These *daily adjustments* need only be subtle. You might describe the process as nothing more than balancing. You're balancing your setup position, shot selection and course management to the swing motion you're creating on a given day. **It's an important aspect of the game that few players even think about.**

How you change your course management is pretty straightforward. On a poor ball-striking day you make a conscious effort to play more conservatively. With regards to shot selection, if you don't have a particular shot on a given day, don't play it. Don't struggle with it, just take it out of your game. I've watched many PGA professionals when struggling with their driver, just leave it in the bag and play a three wood for the balance of the round. I've also watched a touring professional play a fade through an entire round because *on that given day* he was having difficulty drawing the ball.

Making adjustments to your setup position is not as simple. It's an acquired ability that improves over time. You have to learn the approach that works best for you.

In his book, *Natural Golf,* Seve Ballesteros, (before outlining each aspect of his setup position) writes, *"All of these factors, however, are subject to change, which is why it is crucial, when you warm up before a round, to try to identify changes in your swing, either by feel or by studying the ball's flight, or a combination of the two. Then, go ahead and move the ball around in your stance until you find the best positions for playing the various clubs..."*

Without getting technical, making an adjustment to your setup position will involve some version of the following three steps.

Establish a consistent starting point and learn how to get there.

The success of the process is dependent on your ability to correctly perceive a subtle change in your swing motion that's affecting your impact dynamics.

That can only be done from the perspective of a consistent starting point - when you're properly setup to the ball, correctly aligned and swinging at your natural tempo.

The next time you're at a PGA Tour event, visit the practice tee and observe the players warming up before their round. They'll be working on their alignment, setup position, and tempo – their starting point. From this position they're able to best evaluate their impact dynamics on that particular day.

Learn how to correctly *evaluate the feedback* you receive after every swing.

Every time you swing, you get immediate feedback. Through observing your divot, ball flight and the impact location on the clubface, you'll be able to determine how you brought the clubhead to impact.

Remember, when warming-up, keep your focus not on how you should be making contact (whatever that means), but on how you are making contact today (which is the only thing that is important). In his book, *Making The Turn*, PGA Senior Touring Professional Frank Beard writes about the importance of asking yourself, *"How do I feel today?"* *"Who am I today?"* *"What's going on today?"*

Learn how to (if needed) balance your setup position to your swing motion.

If after you've assumed your starting point, you're unhappy with how you're making contact, it's because on that day – for some unexplainable reason - your swing motion is slightly off balance or out-of-sync. At that point, most golfers try to force the issue. They attempt to manipulate their swing motion in an effort to force it into balance with their setup position. **It's much easier to make a slight adjustment to your setup position and play with the swing motion you're producing.**

Just a subtle change in your setup position can positively influence your ball flight. Again, all you're doing is making a very minor adjustment to your starting point to bring it into balance with the swing motion you're making on that particular day.

Your swing motion is not nearly as inconsistent as you think. When your swing moves out of balance, it will tend to do so in a predictable manner. When you learn more about your swing tendencies, you'll find the process of making subtle daily adjustments much easier. The process will become almost natural.

The bottom line is that even the best players in the world, playing with the best fit equipment, will, if needed, make changes to their setup position, equipment and course strategy on a daily basis. Think about that the next time someone tells you that you always have to do this or always have to do that.

In golf, you never always have to do anything. Golf is not about forcing perfect mechanical repetition. Golf is about conforming to changing circumstances. As Byron Nelson once said, *"The only thing you should force is the club back in your bag."*

If my golf swing is always going to change, why should I practice?

You practice primarily to gain confidence and to solidify your shotmaking routine.

The key to better golf is learning to play the game with *more confidence* and a *higher degree of purpose.* Both are acquired through practice.

Knowing that you've successfully executed a particular shot numerous times on the practice tee, gives you the ability to make a *more confident swing* on the golf course.

Hitting practice shots *one shot at a time* makes it much easier to play golf *one shot at a time.*

The goal is to meld the *controllable* aspects of shotmaking into an effective and easily repeatable personal routine. When you employ that routine to hit each practice shot, you'll be *practicing* playing golf with a higher degree of purpose.

In his book, *Golf My Way,* Jack Nicklaus writes, *"All my life I've tried to hit practice shots with great care. I try to have a clear-cut purpose in mind on every swing. I always practice as I intend to play."*

Over 100 years ago, five-time British Open champion, James Braid wrote, *"For practice to have full value, make each swing with the care of a stroke from a tee on medal day."*

You should even *approach* practice sessions exactly as you would *approach* playing a round of golf. First you warm up and analyze the swing motion you're creating on that given day. Then, if needed, you balance your setup position to the swing motion you're creating. After that, you hit practice balls exactly as if you were playing golf – *one shot at a time.* That would require:

Always determining the exact shot you're attempting to create.

Golf is not about hitting it out there somewhere, but that's how most golfers practice. Through always hitting to a very specific target, you practice fine tuning your focus.

Strengthen your intention to create that exact shot.

You need to develop some technique to strengthen your intention. It might be visualizing the ball flight, visualizing the ball's final resting place, verbalizing your objective, or feeling your intention through practice swings. The technique is irrelevant. Just determine which technique works best for you and apply it to each practice shot. The object is to make the step of strengthening your intention an habitual part of your on course approach to each shot.

Insure that you're properly setup to the ball and aligned to the target.

This requires that you develop some type of routine you can use to properly align yourself and assume the correct address position on every shot. Through applying that routine to each practice shot, it will eventually become automatic.

Create the intention of square and centered contact and keep it there until the swing motion is complete.

The intention of making square and centered contact should be applied to *every shot* and it should be *maintained throughout the swing motion.* Through practice, you can train your mind to hold that intention.

Feel as though your natural tempo was initiating and guiding your entire swing motion.

You have to take conscious manipulation out of the golf swing. That requires *trusting* your body. And that *trust* is acquired through practice.

Trying to copy someone else's *approach to shotmaking* is as pointless as trying to copy someone else's swing. You need to determine which techniques work best for you and, through practice, make them habitual. Pia Nilsson and Lynn Marriott wrote in their book, *Every Shot Must Have A Purpose,* *"You first create your habits and then your habits become you. Control what your habits become."*

The *quality* of practice time is far more important than the *quantity.* You can accomplish far more in an hour of quality practice, than a full day of just hitting golf balls *out there somewhere.* I've often heard that it wasn't the amount of golf balls that Hogan hit during his practice sessions that was so impressive, but rather the attention he gave to each shot. He once said, *"While I am practicing I am also trying to develop my powers of concentration. I never just walk up and hit the ball. I am practicing and adopting habits of concentration which pay off when I play...Adopt a habit of concentration to the exclusion of everything else around you on the practice tee and you will find that you are automatically following the same routine while playing a round in competition. Play each shot as if it were part of an actual round.*

A few points to remember about playing better golf

36-time PGA Tour winner and 2-time Vardon trophy winner, Lloyd Mangrum once said, *"There must be a hundred guys out here who can hit the ball farther than me, and fifty who can hit it straighter. Maybe five can putt better, but they can't 'Play' like I can"*.

Here are a few points to remember about *playing* better golf.

- **You don't know how to play golf nearly as well as you think you do. Even with your current equipment and physical ability, your average score would be lower (possibly significantly lower) if you just knew how to *play the game better*.**

- **You don't need to hit more great shots to lower your average score. You just need to replace a few penalizing shots with average shots. *And you can start doing that immediately*.**

- **You'll hit fewer penalizing shots when you learn to play each shot with a *higher degree of purpose*, when you learn to play golf *one shot at a time*.**

- **The essence of good golf is *distance control*, not raw distance. The long hitter's advantage will always be relative to his ability to *control* his distances.**

- **You achieve distance control through playing with golf clubs that *promote distance control* and focusing more on *quality contact* than swing mechanics and clubhead speed.**

- Whether you're stroking a putt, hitting a chip, or making a full swing, your primary goal should always be the same – *square and centered contact*.

- When you always aim at the flag, you'll hit into *penalizing situations* more often and your average score will be higher.

- On every hole, the most important shot will always be the one you're playing.

- Before addressing the ball, you should have already formed an *exact, clear and positive intention* to create a *specific shot*.

- The golf ball, golf club, your body, your swing, and the golf course all exist in the present moment. Your mind, however, could be anywhere. Since all creation takes place in the present moment, that's where your mind should be fully engaged.

- While the shot is being played, you stay present through being *aware and fully engaged* in what you're doing without *thinking about* what you're doing.

- You create the *intention* of making square and centered contact, *focus* on the ball and let your body *effortlessly* respond to your intention.

- Your swing will always unfold best when allowed to do so in the most natural and spontaneous manner, free from the interference of conscious thought.

- Your focus should always support your intention. During your shotmaking routine, you focus first on the target to *support your intention* of getting properly set up to the ball. Then you focus on the ball to *support your intention* of making square and centered contact.

- Fear will always be the greatest hazard in golf. It arises when your mind jumps into the future and considers the consequences of what *might happen*. You may not be able to avoid it, but you can certainly learn how to deal with it.

- You can't improve until you stop trying to *manipulate* your swing motion. You have to accept that your body is smarter than you are and *let go.*

- To say there is nothing you can do about severe mis-hits is like saying there is nothing you can do about losing your focus. We may all periodically lose our focus, *but we can certainly learn to focus better.*

- Good golf requires the ability to create singled-minded focus during the few seconds it takes to execute a golf shot. That focus needs to be centered *exclusively* on the areas within your control.

- Improvement in any area of your game will be limited by your *belief in your ability.* Sometimes the only way to break through a *limiting belief system* is through learning a significantly different technique and developing a completely new perspective and feel for the shot you've been struggling with. In doing so, you might be able to leave the old technique, and all the negative thoughts tied to it, behind you.

- Day-to-day consistency cannot be obtained through making a permanent change in your swing motion. It can only be achieved through learning how to manage the subtle day-to-day changes in your swing motion that will always occur.

- You can manage the subtle daily changes in your swing motion through making subtle changes in your setup position, shot selection and course strategy.

- The key to better golf is learning to play *each shot* with *more confidence* and *a higher degree of purpose.* You can acquire that ability through practicing with a *higher degree of purpose.*

Conclusion

Why the average golfer will never improve and how you can.

Golfers will forever be influenced by golf industry hype. They'll continue to buy the newest golf club designs, continue to change their golf swing, and never improve. That's why the average handicap has never dropped and never will. As Albert Einstein once said, *"I think the definition of insanity is hoping to get a different result by doing the same thing over and over again. We can't solve problems by using the same kind of thinking we used when we created them."*

You, however, don't have to follow the crowd. Regardless of your level of play, you can start lowering your average score immediately. The first step is to forget about golf industry hype. Then, make it your *intention* to score lower, and focus on:

Improving your shot selection

Acquiring the habit of always forming an exact and positive intention *before* addressing the ball.

Establishing a routine that will enable you to get properly set up to the ball and aligned to the target a higher percentage of time.

Learning how to swing at your natural tempo, in balance and free of thought.

Learning how to balance your setup position to your swing motion on a daily basis.

Acquiring a set of golf clubs with which you're able to improve your distance *control*.

Improving your distance control from within 100 yards of the hole.

Improving your ability to *stay present* while on the golf course.

If you stay focused *exclusively* on these areas, your average score will drop – I guarantee it! Thanks for reading my book and I'll look forward to hearing about your progress. You can contact me through my web site, Madsciencegolf.com.

Recommended reading

I always encourage golfers to start their own golf library. I have hundreds of books that I'm constantly referring to and enjoy rereading. Here are just a few that I'd highly recommend.

On the Golf Swing

The Natural Golf Swing, by George Knudsen

Understanding the Golf Swing, by Manuel de la Torre

Jim Flick on Golf, by Jim Flick

The Golf Swing Simplified, by John Jacobs

Gold Doctor, by John Jacobs

On Playing Golf

Every Shot Must Have a Purpose, by Pia Nilsson & Lynn Marriott

Dave Pelz's Short Game Bible, by Dave Pelz

My Story, by Jack Nicklaus

50 Years of Golfing Wisdom, by John Jacobs

Fearless Golf, by Dr. Gio Valiante

Winning the Battle Within, by Dr. Glen Albaugh

On the Mysteries of the Game

The Legend of Bagger Vance, by Steven Pressfield

Golf in the Kingdom, by Michael Murphy

Surfing the Himalayas, by Frederick Lenz

Zen in the Art of Archery, by Eugen Herrigel

The Power of Now, by Eckhart Tolle

Quantum Golf, by Kjell Enhager

Zen Golf, by Dr. Joe Parent

On the Sweeet Spot, by Dr. Richard keefe

Exploring the "Zone", by Larry Miller

Extraordinary Golf, by Fred Shoemaker

On Golf Club fitting

The Search for the perfect Golf Club, by Tom Wishon

On the Rules of the Game

Golf Rules EXPLAINED, by Peter Dobereiner

LaVergne, TN USA
20 November 2010

205735LV00006B/33/A